RAND

Economic Transformation and the Changing International Economic Environment

Charles Wolf, Jr.

The RAND Graduate School

Preface

The essays collected in this monograph were published between November 1990 and April 1993 as op-ed columns or articles in the *Wall Street Journal*, the *Los Angeles Times*, the *New York Times*, *National Interest*, and *World Monitor*. They are collected here on the premise that the whole may be more interesting and useful than the separate pieces. No changes have been made in the original texts, although in a few cases the text that was published was slightly changed from the original version.

The 17 essays are divided into two parts. The first part, "Transforming Command Systems," addresses both the short-term and long-term problems of transforming the command, militarized economies of Russia and Ukraine into marketized, pluralistic ones. The subjects dealt with in this part include the six basic elements of marketization, the relationship between markets and democracy, Russia's foreign debt, and foreign assistance to Russia and Ukraine.

The second part, "The Changing International Economic Environment," touches on disparate, but sometimes interacting, aspects of the new international economic environment, including the relation between economic and military power, the arms trade, the sources of Japan's economic successes, the growing importance of Asia in the world economy, and the components of Clintonomics. The second section also includes two reviews of books by Richard Nixon and Jeffrey Garten, respectively, that deal with the changing international environment, especially with respect to Asia in general and Japan in particular.

Contents

Figure

I. Transforming Command Systems

1. From There to Here: Transforming Command Economies into Market Economies[1]

Over the past century, economists and other intellectuals have produced an enormous literature on how to convert capitalist market economies into centrally planned, socialist ones. The notable contributors include the Webbs (Sidney and Beatrice), Oskar Lange, Abba Lerner, Joan Robinson, Nicholas Kaldor, Paul Sweezy, Wassily Leontief, J. K. Galbraith, and innumerable others.

It is ironic that the reverse problem of converting socialist economies into capitalist ones has received scant attention. The writings of Friedrich Hayek, Joseph Schumpeter, Milton Friedman, and P. T. Bauer are partial exceptions, but their focus has usually been elsewhere: namely, exposing the errors made by the advocates of socialism, rather than charting the transformation to market economies. Hence, there is no general theory to draw on in addressing the crucial economic policy problem of the 1990s: how to transform command economies into market economies.

Recognition of the failures of command economies, and the need to transform them, is the reason why the rhetoric of "markets" and "marketizing" is definitely "in" in the 1990s. But the unanimity and ubiquity with which markets are advocated—in the Soviet Union and its principal republics, as well as in the countries of Eastern Europe, China, and the Third World—obscure the profound divergences about what the terms mean, and what they imply for transforming command economies into market-oriented ones. These divergences are latent in such frequently used oxymorons as "market socialism" (a term invented by the Hungarian economist, Janos Kornai, but subsequently rejected by him), or "regulated socialist markets" (a term favored periodically by Gorbachev and

---

[1]This essay was published under the title "Getting to Market" by *National Interest* in Spring 1991. Reprinted by permission.

4

certain "conservative" Soviet economists), or what some Chinese leaders envisage as a system between capitalism and socialism, which they describe as "socialism with Chinese characteristics."

The underlying disagreements concern the details about transforming command systems into market systems. In this case, as in others, the details are crucial. They relate to whether markets should be "free" or "regulated," competitive or "social"; whether the market's intended reach should be extensive and predominant, or partial and limited; whether transformation should be rapid or gradual; whether the emergent system should be open to international competition and should allow free movement of capital and commodities, or be protected from them; and, finally, whether the scope of the government sector, at the end of the process, should be extensive, or narrowly circumscribed.

That these divergences are so deep is not surprising. The rhetoric of markets and marketizing has been adopted by a remarkably diverse group of advocates, including Communists, ex-Communists, erstwhile central planners, Social Democrats, "liberals," and "radicals," as well as new and aspiring entrepreneurs in the transforming command economies. The advocates also include an ideologically mixed set of experts, advisers, consultants, and commentators in the West, including some—like Jacques Delors, Secretary General of the European Community, and Jacques Attali, head of the new Bank for European Reconstruction and Development—who have until recently favored transformation of capitalist economies into socialist ones.

As a result of this diversity of views and viewers, the ensuing policy debate has often been muddled, the essentials of the transformation process frequently misunderstood, and its costs generally exaggerated. Indeed, transforming command (or "non-market") economies into market ones, although a challenging problem, is more tractable, and the costs and "pain" of the transition should be considerably less, than much of the debate has implied—provided the transformation is pursued comprehensively and aggressively.

Transformation as a Systems Problem

The generic problems of transforming a command economy into a market economy are essentially the same whether the locale is the Soviet Union, Eastern Europe, China, or many of the centrally controlled economies of the Third World. To be sure, there are differences in historical circumstances, cultural affinities, institutional antecedents, and the existing physical, social, and political infrastructures. But the differences are incidental to an essentially similar task. Transformation depends on implementing simultaneously, or at least contemporaneously, a package of six closely linked and mutually supporting elements:

- Monetary reform to ensure control of the money supply and credit.

- Fiscal control to assure budgetary balance and to limit monetization of a budget deficit if one occurs.

- Price and wage deregulation, to link prices and wages to costs and productivity, respectively.

- Privatization, legal protection of property rights, and the breakup of state monopolies, to provide for competition, as well as worker and management incentives that reflect changes in relative market prices.

- A social "safety net" to protect those who may become unemployed as transformation proceeds.

- Currency convertibility to link the transforming economy to the world economy and to competition in international markets.

These six elements are mutually supporting and interactive. The first two—monetary reform and fiscal control—and the fifth—the social safety net—create the broad macroeconomic environment that enables the incentive mechanisms of the other three elements to move resources toward more efficient and growth-promoting uses. The government's role is both crucial and paradoxical: crucial in initiating all of the elements, yet paradoxical because the process that the government initiates is intended to diminish its ensuing role, displacing its overextended functions and reducing its size in favor of market mechanisms.

Each of the six elements is less likely to be effective without the reciprocal support provided by the other elements. Hence, attempts to reform non-market economies by piecemeal steps are more likely to founder than to succeed.

Consider, for example, the link between the first two elements. Monetary reform is necessary to limit growth of the money supply to a rate that accords with the growth of real output. It is also a necessary means to provide access to credit on the basis of borrowers' economic capabilities and their associated risks, rather than on the basis of their political connections or credentials. A competent entrepreneur with a good idea should be able to obtain credit that is not available to someone whose principal distinction is membership in the governing political party or kinship to a government official.

Fiscal reform requires a budget process that constrains government expenditures to a level approximating that of revenues, and precludes or limits "off-budget" subsidies and other transactions that would disrupt monetary discipline, as well as budgetary balance. Recourse to extra-budgetary subsidies to bail out deficit-ridden state enterprises has been a standard procedure in the Soviet Union, China, and other command economies. Fiscal and monetary reform should preclude its recurrence. Usually, the complementarity between monetary reform and fiscal reform is facilitated by institutional separation between the Finance Ministry (or Treasury), and the Central Bank or banking system.

In turn, the third element—deregulation of prices and wages—requires monetary and fiscal restraint if deregulation is to change relative prices by linking them, as well as wages, to real costs and productivity, while avoiding general inflation. Goods that are in short supply or are costly to produce should experience price increases relative to those that are more abundant and less costly. In turn, these price increases provide signals and incentives for increased and more efficient production. Similarly, wages paid for more productive labor and skills should be expected to rise relative to those that are less productive. Moreover, the newly established parities among costs and prices should operate in the public sector, as well as the private sector.

For deregulation of prices and wages to promote efficient use of resources requires contemporaneous implementation of the fourth element: privatization, legal protection of property rights, and the breakup of state monopolies into competing entities. This requires an appropriate legal code and appropriate procedures for resolving disputes over property transactions and acquisitions. It also requires a choice among several alternative ways of changing from state ownership to private ownership—an issue on which there is considerable controversy among policymakers, economists, lawyers, and financiers.

For example, equity shares in state enterprises can be issued to enterprise workers and management, while reserving some proportion of the shares for local government and foreign investors, as well as providing for resale of the shares with or without a specified holding period. This method, favored by Paul Roberts among others, has the advantage of simplicity and clarity; its putative disadvantage is the ostensible unfairness of a process in which some of the new shareholders would be losers, while others would realize gains, due in both cases to the arbitrary circumstance of where they had been previously employed.

Another mode of privatization is to issue enterprise shares to the general public on a random basis, rather than determining enterprise ownership on the basis of employment. In this case, everyone has an equal chance of picking a winner or loser among the hundreds or thousands of state enterprises that typically exist in the command economies. Windfall gains that result from a random process are, it can be argued, more equitable than those that result from the accident of prior employment.

Perhaps the simplest method of privatization is to auction enterprises to their highest bidders—limiting or excluding participation by non-nationals. This method, favored by Czechoslovakian economist (and Finance Minister) Vaclav Klaus, as well as others, has sometimes been criticized on the grounds that those most likely to have ample funds enabling them to win the bidding are the black marketeers and former Communist Party *nomenklatura*.

Still another method is to issue vouchers to the public representing potential claims on the shares of enterprises to be privatized, and then to invite foreign bankers or mutual fund managers to bid for the public vouchers, on the basis of the portfolio selection criteria favored by the competing funds. The public would surrender their vouchers in return for shares in the mutual funds that appealed to individual voucher holders. Variants of this method of privatization have been advanced by Jeff Sachs and several Polish economists.

All of these methods would result in the creation of a resale market for equities and mutual fund shares. Contrary to some of the debate on this issue, none of the methods requires that state enterprises be carefully evaluated *before* privatization is accomplished. Choosing among the alternative methods requires assessment of their respective advantages (for example, simplicity, comprehensibility, and speed), as well as their disadvantages (for example, distributional unfairness and inequity).

In any event, whichever method or methods of privatization are selected—and experimentation with several is advisable because none is clearly preferable to the others—their success remains linked to the other elements of the transformation package. Unless rewards are linked to asset ownership, and unless such rewards can be accumulated legally, incentives to innovate and to increase productivity will be impaired. Effective supply responses to price and wage deregulation depend on the incentives provided by private ownership and accumulation. Moreover, private ownership is essential for market forces to provide an effective "stick," as well as "carrot." If ownership is in the hands of the state, the discipline imposed by market competition will be attenuated, if not eliminated. When state enterprises are confronted by losses, they typically evade or ignore the threat of bankruptcy that private enterprises would face if confronted by similar losses.

It has sometimes been argued—by Gorbachev in the Soviet Union and Li Peng in China, as well as by others both inside and outside the reforming command economies—that privatization is neither necessary nor would it be effective. The contention accompanying this argument is that privatization leads to wide gaps between rich and poor, and that a "culture of envy" has become strongly pervasive and ingrained, especially in the Soviet Union. Consequently, it is argued, privatization won't be tolerated, and won't be effective if it is imposed.

To the extent these attitudes exist, they may be attributable to long-standing and widespread experience that sharp disparities in income distribution, and in levels of living, have been associated with political preferment or corruption, rather than with private ownership, innovation, and productivity. Resentment against the sharp disparities prevailing in command Communist systems has been due to the widespread conviction that the rich and powerful have acquired their positions through political clout or favoritism, rather than economic innovation or productivity. Such resentment is not unknown in market economies. Nevertheless, in moving from command to market economies, private ownership plays a crucial role by providing the incentive structure required for markets to function efficiently. To avoid socially unacceptable disparities in income distribution is a responsibility of public expenditure and tax policies, within the context of private ownership and market competition.

The fifth element—establishment of a social security system as a "safety net"—is also essential for the transformation process to succeed. Without it, the process as a whole may create a fear of widespread unemployment (although I will suggest later why increased unemployment, when accurately measured, may be considerably less than what has been feared), as well as social stress, political instability, and a serious impediment to the transition to a market system.

In most command economies, social protection—against illness, disability, age, and unemployment—has principally been the responsibility of state enterprises. As privatization proceeds, these responsibilities are likely to become one of the principal functions of government, financed by taxation as well as by payments levied on the insured. In the initial stage of transformation, taxation will probably have to bear most of the burden although, for reasons to be discussed later, the real *incremental* burden imposed on the economy by the social safety net is likely to be less than is usually assumed.

The final element—currency convertibility—is essential to complete the transformation process by linking internal markets and their prices, wages, productivities, and technologies, to those of international markets. This linkage provides the opportunity for comparative costs and comparative advantage to operate for the benefit of the transforming national economy. By having a convertible currency, the transforming economy can determine those goods and services it can produce at relatively low cost compared to the costs of other countries, and those it produces at relatively high cost. In response to convertibility, exports of the relatively low-cost goods will expand, as will imports of the relatively high-cost ones.

If the other elements of the package—especially monetary and fiscal discipline, and market-determined prices—are effectively implemented, currency convertibility with a floating exchange rate can be embarked upon and sustained with minimal hard currency reserves, contrary to a frequent argument about the need for large reserves as a precondition for convertibility. Poland's establishment of a convertible zloty at the beginning of 1990 was accomplished notwithstanding the country's net foreign exchange indebtedness of over $50 billion! Although Poland received a foreign exchange stabilization loan of $1 billion from the United States, none of it was drawn upon in the ensuing year. Instead, with its convertible currency system, Poland accumulated hard currency foreign exchange holdings of over $2 billion in the ensuing year.

The interactions and mutually supporting relationships among the six elements of the transformation process are summarized in Figure 1. The solid lines indicate the contribution by one element to the effectiveness of another element to which the arrowhead points. (For example, monetary and fiscal reform contribute reciprocally to supporting one another, while both of them contribute to the effectiveness of price and wage deregulation.)

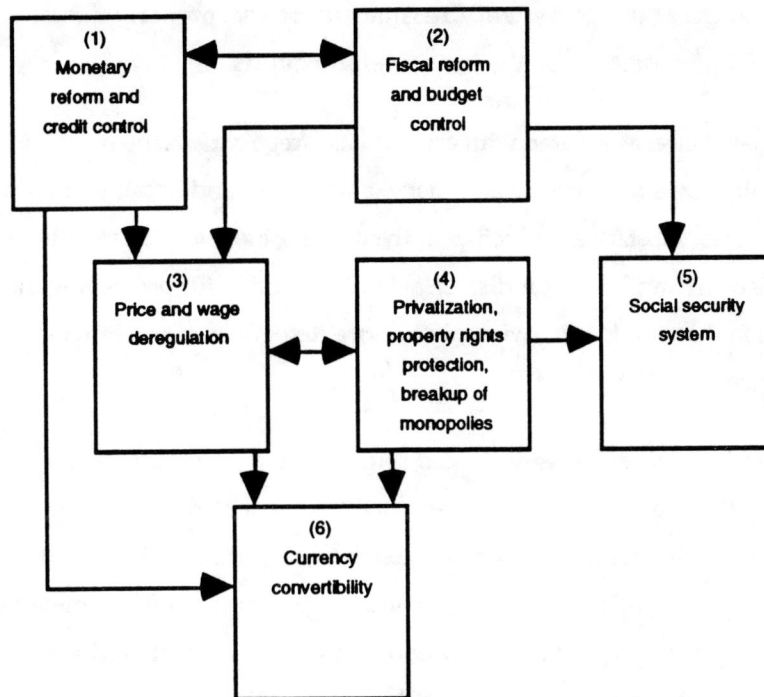

Figure 1—Components of Transformation of Command Economies

In sum, the process of transforming command, non-market economies to market economies is both better understood and more tractable than might be inferred from much of the public debate. Transformation is a systems process encompassing all of the interactive and mutually supporting elements described above. The debate which disputes this systems view argues instead that one or another of the six elements is not essential, or is of higher priority than other elements, or should precede the others.

For example, as noted earlier, Gorbachev in the Soviet Union, Li Peng in China, and some of their "conservative" advisers, contend that private ownership of productive assets, including land, is inessential, while its incentive effects can be obtained through leases administered by the state. In opposition to this view is the position of American banker Leif Olsen, Soviet economist Nikolai Shmelev, and others, who assert that private ownership in general and privatization of state enterprises in particular are the most fundamental ingredients of economic restructuring. Along the same line, Canadian economist Reuven Brenner argues that reform of the legal system, to assure and protect property rights, is the essential precondition for any further reform efforts.

Another stance, associated with economists Gregory Grossman, Igor Birman, and Judy Shelton, emphasizes the primacy of monetary and fiscal reform and, in the Soviet case, substantial reduction of the existing monetary stock—the so-called "ruble overhang"—as an indispensable precondition for preventing the rampant inflation that would otherwise follow price deregulation and other reform measures.

Indeed, I have previously advanced some of these views myself. In earlier writings on the Soviet Union, I suggested that price and wage deregulation, combined with the mandatory conversion of large ruble holdings into long-term, non-tradable bonds, were necessary and sufficient measures for moving the Soviet economy toward marketization. And in subsequent work on China, I focused on the central importance of currency convertibility in achieving marketization. Now, it seems clear to me, for both theoretical and practical reasons, that trying to transform a command system into a market system without the synergy provided by all of these elements is like trying to swim with one arm and leg rather than two of each. To attempt the transformation process on a piecemeal and gradual basis would be—to use another simile—like trying to shift a country's driving practices from the left side of the road to the right side in stages. The risk of serious accident is manifestly greater than if the change is accomplished all at once.

Some Recent Experience

Among the command economies that have attempted to transform themselves into market economies, Poland's efforts have been the most far-reaching. Yet these changes—although more extensive and effective than restructuring efforts elsewhere—have been incomplete. On the positive side, Poland's budget deficit has been reduced from approximately 8 percent to about 1 percent of GNP.

Monetary discipline has been encouraged by separating the Central Bank from the Treasury. Ninety percent of all prices have been decontrolled, and convertibility of the zloty has been maintained at a stable rate since January 1990, with exports increasing, hard currency imports declining, and a resulting trade surplus of over $2 billion.

These are significant accomplishments, although not sufficient. To date, the Poles have only partially privatized. They have deferred the breaking up of state monopolies and delayed the wage reform necessary to create proper incentives for labor and management. Hence, supply responses and sectoral resource reallocations have been inhibited, and output, employment, and inflation have suffered. Still, if one were grading the various country efforts, Poland would receive a strong B.

By contrast, Gorbachev's faltering attempts to move toward a market economy, and to combine the defunct Ryzhkov and Shatalin plans, would barely rate a D. Thus far, controls remain on the prices of essential consumer goods, as well as basic commodities like oil, gas, lumber, steel, and other key goods and services, such as transportation and communications. Although their "established" or official prices have been raised, the levels and parities among them are determined by central planners, not by the market. Budgetary spending is supposed to be curtailed, yet subsidies for many enterprises have been maintained. State enterprises are supposed to resort to "self-financing" to an increasing extent to meet their financial needs. In fact, credit extensions evidently are available to them if stringencies arise, especially if the enterprises can argue that financing is needed to fulfill state contracts. Although state enterprises are intended to be privatized, no timetable or operational plan for doing so has been established. And to the extent that convertibility of the ruble is mentioned at all, the intention is that it will be "gradual," without any indication of when or how this will be accomplished. And even these limited measures have been set back as a result of the recent increased reliance on KGB and military authority in running the economy.

China's economic restructuring efforts probably rank somewhere between Poland and the Soviet Union—perhaps warranting a grade of C, probably higher for its rural reform in the early 1980s, but lower than C for its meager reform efforts in the urban sector before and after the Tiananmen tragedy of June 1989. While there has been extensive price deregulation, wages remain largely fixed. Limited progress has been made in the direction of privatization, especially through joint ventures with foreign investors. State enterprises remain largely responsible for social security, thereby burdening them with high cost obligations and impeding any prospective progress toward the breaking up and privatization of these enterprises. Although there has been no explicit move toward convertibility, the establishment of fairly effective monetary and fiscal discipline has helped to create a situation in which the black market value of the ren min bi is only about 30 percent below the official rate.

Transitional Costs of Transformation

It is widely assumed in much of the ongoing debate that the transitional costs of transforming command economies into market ones will be extremely high, as well as protracted. But this assessment is flawed by a fundamental measurement error. In fact, the costs and pain of the transition are likely to be less than is usually presumed, if the process is pursued along the inclusive and expeditious lines described earlier.

The critical error arises from comparing real levels of output, employment, and prices in the post-transformation market environment with the spurious recorded levels of the prior command environment. For example, it has been said that Poland's GNP has declined by 16 percent, unemployment has risen to more than one million, and inflation has increased by 35 percent more than wages since Poland's "crash" economic reform program was initiated in January 1990. Similar or greater disruptions have been forecast by Gorbachev and others in the Soviet Union if "radical" restructuring were to proceed there. All of these figures are wide of the mark.

In non-market systems, like that of the Soviet Union, or China, or Poland prior to 1990, recorded output is typically and substantially overestimated due to several factors: (1) underestimation of "hidden" inflation that takes the form of maintaining constant prices for products of decreasing quality, or establishing higher prices for products that are reclassified to reflect apparent, but not actual, increases in quality (in the Soviet Union, it has recently been estimated that the annual rate of inflation in recent years has probably been two or three times the previously accepted rate of about two percent); (2) inclusion of physical, but valueless, output—for example, shoes that consumers won't buy, bulldozers that are too hazardous to use and too costly to fix; (3) fraudulent reporting—the padding of reported data (*pripiski*) to meet or exceed established production norms; and (4) data manipulation for internal or external propaganda purposes.

Such factors probably account for overestimates of at least 25 percent of recorded GNP in the Soviet Union and other non-market systems. It is significant that estimates of the size of the Soviet GNP relative to that of the United States by the CIA (as well as by the State Committee on Statistics in the Soviet Union) have placed the figure at about 50 percent, whereas estimates by other economists— Soviet as well as American and European—have placed the figure between 14 percent and about 30 percent! The 14 percent estimate is by academician Vladimir Tikhonov, and Victor Belkin. Soviet economists Vasili Selyunin and Grigorii Khanin have placed the figure at about 20 to 25 percent, and Anders Aslund and Igor Birman have estimated it at about 30 percent.[2] It is also significant that East Germany's per capita GNP in 1987 was estimated by both the CIA and the World Bank at about 88 percent of West Germany's, while more accurate estimates since unification suggest a figure of less than 50 percent!

Similarly, comparisons between post-transformation and pre-transformation unemployment are misleading because they are based on unemployment that is visible in the market economy, but do not allow for the make-work, featherbedding, and pay-without-product unemployment that is hidden in the pre-transformation, non-market system. The employment realities are suggested by the familiar Soviet joke: "We pretend to work, and they pretend to pay us."

---

[2]See my testimony before the Senate Foreign Relations Committee, "Estimating the Size and Growth of the Soviet Economy," July 16, 1990. See also, Henry S. Rowen and Charles Wolf, Jr., (eds.), *The Impoverished Superpower: Perestroika and the Soviet Military Burden*, ICS Press, San Francisco, 1990, especially Chapter 1 by Anders Aslund, "How Small is Soviet National Income?"

Finally, it is misleading to compare post-transformation "inflation" with pre-transformation's apparent price stability. Transformation to a market system converts inflation that has typically been "hidden" in the non-market system—but reflected in long and uncertain queues, as well as declining product quality—into visible price increases in the market system.

When properly measured, the economic costs of the transition—in the accurate sense of opportunity costs—should be much less than suggested by most comments and estimates.

Why Is Transformation Faltering?

If transformation to a market system is more tractable and the attendant costs are likely to be lower than is commonly assumed, why has progress been lacking (as in the Soviet Union), or very limited (as in China), or at best only modest (as in Poland)?

The question relates rather more to the politics than to the economics of transformation, more to the motivation and capacity of potential leadership and organizations than to understanding the policies necessary for moving forward. Part of the answer lies in the fact that there are deep underlying divergences among many of those who intone free market rhetoric and slogans, but are themselves decidedly ambivalent about the desirability of real system transformation. Hence, they seek reasons or excuses for delaying and temporizing, even while solemnly acknowledging the necessity for eventual systemic change. To profess a belief in free markets together with an intention of maintaining the political dominance of the Communist Party, as does the leadership of both the Soviet Union and China, is an oxymoron.

Transforming command economies into market economies inevitably means winners and losers, although in the aggregate, the economy will gain more than it loses. In the Soviet Union, the issue is further complicated by the likelihood that the economy that gains will be that of the republics, while the loser will be that of the union. The practical problem created by impending transformation is that the reigning leaders in the ostensibly transforming economies—the Soviet

17

Union, China, Romania, Bulgaria—are very likely to be among the losers in terms of their power, privilege, and prestige, as well as those of their principal associates. Hence, while they may use the rhetoric of markets and competition, their interests induce, if not compel, them to temporize, to delay, and perhaps to incapacitate the transformation process.

2. Transforming Command Economies into Market Economies[3]

It is widely believed that the transitional costs of transforming the command economies of Eastern Europe, the Soviet Union, and China into market economies will be extremely high, as well as protracted. But this assessment is flawed by a fundamental measurement error. In fact, the costs and pain of the transition are likely to be considerably less than is usually presumed, provided the transformation is pursued comprehensively and aggressively.

The error arises from comparing *real* levels of output, employment, and prices in the post-transformation market environment with the *spurious* recorded levels of the prior command environment. For example, it is said that Poland's GNP has declined by 16 percent, unemployment has risen to 1 million, and inflation has risen by 35 percent more than wages since Poland's "crash" economic program was initiated in January 1990. Similar or greater disruptions have been forecast by Gorbachev and Ryzhkov if "radical" restructuring were to proceed in the Soviet Union.

All of these figures are wide of the mark.

In non-market systems, like that of the Soviet Union or of Poland prior to 1990, recorded output is typically overestimated due to several factors: failure to allow for deterioration in product quality that predictably occurs when enterprise performance depends on meeting quantitative norms rather than producing net market value; inclusion of physical, but valueless, output (for example, shoes that consumers won't buy, bulldozers that are too hazardous to use and too costly to fix); fraudulent reporting—the padding of reported data (*"pripiski"*)—to meet or exceed norms; data manipulation for propaganda purposes; and so on.

---

[3]A slightly abbreviated version of this essay was published under the title "Less Pain, More Gain for the East Bloc" by the *Wall Street Journal* on November 19, 1990. Reprinted by permission of The Wall Street Journal, © 1990 Dow Jones & Company, Inc. All Rights Reserved Worldwide.

Such factors probably account for overestimates of at least 25 percent in recorded GNP in the Soviet Union and other non-market systems. Significantly, East Germany's per capita GNP in 1987 was estimated by the CIA and the World Bank at 88 percent of West Germany's, while more accurate recent estimates suggest a figure of less than 50 percent!

Similarly, comparisons between post-transformation and pre-transformation unemployment are misleading because they are based on unemployment that is *visible* in the market economy, but do not allow for the make-work, featherbedding, and pay-without-product unemployment that is *hidden* in the pre-transformation, non-market system. The realities are suggested by the familiar Soviet joke: "we pretend to work, and they pretend to pay us!"

Finally, it is misleading to compare post-transformation "inflation" with pre-transformation's apparent price stability. Transformation to a market system converts inflation that has typically been "hidden" in the non-market system— but reflected in long and uncertain queues, as well as declining product quality— into *visible* price increases in the market regime.

In sum, the usual estimates of the economic costs of transforming non-market to market systems are distorted because they compare exaggerated estimates of pre-transformation economic performance with more accurate estimates of post-transformation performance. The real economic value of Poland's current GNP probably equals or exceeds that of the prior non-market, command system.

Although the usual estimates exaggerate the transitional costs associated with transformation to a market system, the challenge of effectively transforming command economies to market economies remains formidable—formidable but tractable. Its tractability depends on implementing jointly a package of six mutually supporting elements: monetary reform, to ensure control of credit and the money supply; fiscal control, to assure budgetary balance and to limit monetization of a budget deficit if one arises; price and wage deregulation, to link prices and wages to costs and productivity; privatization, legal protection of property rights, and breakup of state monopolies, to provide entrepreneurial and labor incentives that reflect changing market prices; a social "safety net," to protect those who may become unemployed as transformation proceeds; and currency convertibility, to link the transforming economy to the world economy and to competition in international markets.

These elements are mutually supporting and interactive: the first two create the macroeconomic environment that enables the incentive mechanisms of the other elements to move resources toward more efficient uses.

Each of the six elements is less likely to be effective without the reciprocal support provided by the other elements.

For example, if prices are deregulated without simultaneously establishing control of the money supply and imposing fiscal restraint, inflation and inconvertibility will result. If, as in Poland, both monetary and budgetary control are established, prices freed, and convertibility introduced but privatization and the breakup of state monopolies are deferred, the transformation's effectiveness will be impaired. And without the necessary social safety net, the other measures may create a fear of widespread unemployment, social stress, and political instability.

Trying to transform a non-market to a market system without the synergy provided by all six elements is like trying to swim with one arm and leg rather than two of each.

Gorbachev's current attempt to combine the Ryzhkov and Shatalin plans scores poorly when viewed in this light. Controls would remain on prices of essential consumer goods, basic commodities like oil and gas, and other "key" goods and services, such as transportation and communications. Budgetary spending would be curtailed, but subsidies for many enterprises would be maintained. State enterprises are intended to be privatized, but no timetable or operational plan for doing so is established. Convertibility of the ruble is to be "gradual," without any indication of when or how.

By way of contrast, Poland's efforts at systemic transformation have been much more far-reaching than what is planned in the Soviet Union. Yet even Poland's changes have been insufficiently inclusive. On the positive side, fiscal discipline has been imposed and the budget deficit has been reduced from approximately 8 percent to 1 percent of GNP. Monetary discipline has been encouraged by separating the Central Bank from the Treasury. Ninety percent of all prices have been decontrolled, and convertibility of the zloty has been maintained at a stable rate since January 1990, with exports increasing, hard currency imports declining, and a resulting trade surplus of over $2 billion.

These are significant accomplishments, but they are not sufficient. To date, the Poles have only partially privatized. They have deferred the breaking up of state monopolies and delayed the wage reform necessary to create proper incentives for workers and managers. Hence, supply responses and sectoral resource reallocations have been inhibited, and output, employment, and inflation have suffered.

Still, if transformation to a market system is more tractable and the attendant costs are lower than is commonly assumed, why has progress been lacking (as in the Soviet Union), or limited (as in Poland)?

The question is genuinely puzzling. Part of the answer may be that many members of the unusually diverse chorus of ex-communists, socialists, social democrats, and erstwhile central planners, who intone free market rhetoric, are often decidedly ambivalent about the desirability of real transformation. So they seek reasons or excuses for delaying and temporizing, even while solemnly acknowledging the necessity for eventual systemic change.

3. Democracy and Free Markets[4]

When Boris Yeltsin visits Washington in the middle of June, his hosts will encourage, if not urge, him to proceed aggressively with both democratization and marketization in Russia. Yet the frequent, sometimes bitter and surely recurring disputes between Yeltsin and the Russian parliament are a reminder that the relationship between democratization and marketization is more complex, less predictable, and more conflicted than is often assumed. Contrary to the familiar rhetoric of U.S. policy statements, congressional legislation, and media pronouncements, "democracy" and "free markets" are not synonymous.

To be sure, the two have several significant features in common. Both involve decentralization, devolution, and competition. Free markets decentralize and devolve economic power among competing producers and competing consumers. Democracy decentralizes and devolves political power among competing parties, candidates, and voters.

Nevertheless, the connection between them is not assured. Some democratic polities, like Israel and India, have socialist rather than market-oriented economies. And some market-oriented economies have (or have had for protracted periods) authoritarian, non-democratic polities—for example, South Korea from 1960 through the 1980s, Chile in the 1970s and 1980s, and Singapore, Taiwan, and South China currently.

Reflecting on the relation between democracy and free markets, some (Hayek, Friedman) have argued that the two are mutually dependent and inextricably connected—each requires the other. Others (Lipset) have suggested that the relationship between the two, while mutually supportive, is not determinative— one may occur without the other. And still others (Schumpeter) have argued that

---

[4]A slightly abbreviated version of this essay was published under the title "Yeltsin's Choice— Democracy or Markets" by the *Wall Street Journal* on June 3, 1992. Reprinted by permission of The Wall Street Journal, © 1992 Dow Jones & Company, Inc. All Rights Reserved Worldwide.

the relationship between markets and democracy may well be competitive and conflicting.

The formidable obstacles that the Russian parliament presents for Yeltsin's economic reforms reflect the sometimes conflicted relationship between markets and democracies, but the underlying reasons differ from those which worried Schumpeter. Schumpeter saw the conflict between democracy and free markets arising from the opposing tendencies associated with each of them: on the one hand, the tendency of free market processes to generate large disparities between winners and losers; and, on the other hand, the tendency of democratic processes to take from the winners and redistribute their gains—in the process undermining incentives and substituting central controls and regulations in place of free markets.

Yeltsin's problem is of a different, but not unrelated, sort. It springs from the process of transforming a non-market, command economy into a market economy at the same time as an authoritarian political system is being transformed into a more democratic one. In Russia's case, the conflict arises because the market transformation requires that several essential, as well as interacting, measures must be implemented simultaneously, or at least in close synchronization with one another. These measures involve fiscal and monetary stabilization (a balanced budget and control of the money supply); decontrol of prices and wages; privatization, demonopolization, and free entry of competing new enterprises; currency convertibility; and a suitable social safety net. The monetary and fiscal controls provide the stable macroeconomic environment that enables the microeconomic incentives and mechanisms of the other measures to move resources to more efficient and growth-promoting uses. Because these measures are synergistically connected, the chance that any one will be effective is reduced in the absence of reciprocal support provided by the others.

The rub lies in the unsurprising, although not inevitable, tendency of more or less democratically selected legislatures (the present Russian parliament lies in the "less-democratic" part of this range) to delay, obstruct, and restrict implementation of comprehensive marketizing reforms, and to do so in concert with special interest constituencies. In Russia, these special interests reside in the state enterprises, especially the military-industrial complex, and the bureaucracy—both of which correctly anticipate that they would be big losers in a genuinely free market environment.

Yeltsin has demonstrated remarkable adroitness and political sophistication in coping with these pressures—maintaining at least modest progress toward marketization, while being obliged periodically to backtrack in response to resistance and threats from the so-called "conservative" forces in the Russian parliament. This backtracking is reflected by the recent decisions of the Gaidar government to postpone privatization, to continue large subsidies to non-productive (and often counterproductive) state enterprises, and to maintain huge budget deficits that add to a continually expanding money supply and thereby intensify inflationary pressures.

Where this will lead is unclear. As Sam Goldwyn observed, forecasts are always hazardous—especially about the future.

However, it is doubtful that progress by this oscillatory process—one step backward for each two steps forward—will be sufficient to move the ossified Russian economy toward an effectively functioning market system.

In a Panglossian world, democratization and free markets would progress in step and in harmony, or at least in measured and balanced counterpoint to one another. There would be a "trade-on," rather than a trade-off, between them. Moreover, in the long run the association between democracy and free markets is more assured than in the intervening short runs that comprise it. But in the pressing short run that Yeltsin and his supporters confront, difficult choices may well arise between the demands of market economics and the restraints imposed by democratic politics. Yeltsin's choices may, in turn, face Western policymakers with a dilemma: accepting an abridgment of Russia's inchoate democratization (for example, if Yeltsin's authority to govern by decree is expanded) to sustain the economy's embryonic marketization, or opposing such a trade-off. Neither alternative is without drawbacks, but watchful acceptance is preferable because opposition will probably not advance either democracy or free markets.

4. The Question of Soviet Aid[5]

Aid to the Soviet Union was initially placed on the agenda of the G-7 Summit in Houston in 1990 by France and Germany. It was elevated to the top of the G-7 agenda in London in 1991 by Gorbachev's own appearance there. In the wake of the global euphoria over the aborted 72-hour Moscow coup, the subject has acquired immediate prominence.

Although Gorbachev received less at the London meeting than he asked for, he did not leave empty-handed. He was offered technical assistance to help move the Soviet Union toward a market economy, a recommendation by the G-7 for associate (non-borrowing) Soviet membership in the International Monetary Fund the World Bank, and (from George Bush) the prospect of most-favored-nation access to the U.S. market. He also elicited an implied promise: "full engagement" (implying Western aid) by the G-7 members would depend on clear evidence of Soviet progress in implementing an "irrevocable commitment" to fundamental systemic reform.

Despite its ambiguity, this promise will surely be tested in the coming months, as well as at the 1992 G-7 Summit in Berlin. The ensuing debate will probably strain the Seven's cohesion by pitting its European members against Japan and the United States.

Japan's role is crucial because Japan is the only member of the Seven with a substantial and continuing current account surplus—probably about $50 to $60 billion in 1991—that would enable it to finance large-scale aid. (The German and U.S. current account deficits will be about $25 and $50 billion, respectively.) If G-7 members other than Japan were to provide aid to the Soviet Union, they would be obliged—directly or indirectly—to borrow from Japan, or to sell other assets

---

[5]A slightly abbreviated version of this essay was published under the title "Soviets Need Change, Not Tons of Money" by the *Los Angeles Times* on September 12, 1991.

to it in return for current Japanese funding. Japan would be the ultimate paymaster.

Although Japan's stance would doubtless be heavily influenced by the United States, its reluctance to become "fully engaged" in aiding the Soviet Union has deep roots. They relate not only to its unresolved claims for return by the Soviets of the four Kurile Islands, but to other concerns as well: the powerful and still modernizing Soviet military forces—especially naval, air, and missile forces—in the Okhotsk bastion and in Soviet East Asia; the changing but still uncertain state of Soviet relations with North and South Korea; and the serious Japanese doubts about whether there are realistic prospects of achieving successful economic and political reform in the Soviet Union.

On all of these matters, Japan is the most "conservative" of all the G-7 countries in its coolness toward large-scale aid to the Soviet Union.

The case for large-scale aid from the West entails other fundamental shortcomings, quite apart from Japan's crucial role, and notwithstanding the abundant good will toward the Soviet people and Boris Yeltsin generated by their stalwart resistance to the short-lived Moscow coup.

First, the proposition that concessional government-to-government aid can assist in transforming a non-market system into a market one is an oxymoron. The essence of a market system is that inputs (labor, capital, raw materials) and outputs (goods and services) are exchanged at prices determined by the interaction between market demand and supply. Prices of outputs reflect their scarcity values and production costs, and prices of inputs reflect their productivity (or "opportunity cost") in their best alternative uses.

The essence of concessional aid, on the other hand, is that capital, equipment, and commodities are provided by donors at prices that do not reflect market forces. Government-to-government aid carries with it either no costs or subsidized costs to the recipient, thereby absolving it from having to meet a market test in the use of aid. Whereas genuine marketizing reform requires market-based prices, "aid" means that market prices are deliberately ignored. While marketization implies access to external resources through the competitive international capital market, "aid" implies access through the favors of foreign governments.

To promote marketization by concessional aid is like teaching a child to avoid fires by giving her matches, or reforming an alcoholic by a gift of liquor.

The second flaw is the unavoidable problem of resource fungibility. Providing the Soviet Union with aid resources means that donors cannot be sure what the net effect actually is of the additional resources that are provided. An ostensible "bargain" that purports to relate the added resources to changes in Soviet resource allocations—for example, to cuts in Soviet military spending and forces, as advocated by Martin Feldstein—or to other changes in Soviet behavior, would be an illusory bargain. The reason is that Soviet policymakers already face strong and growing pressures to cut military allocations—pressures that will no doubt be intensified by the recently aborted coup—to scale back or divest the capacity of military industry and to shift it to market-based civil production. Because resources are fungible, concessional assistance will be as likely to abate as to abet these pressures.

Another reason why concessional aid is as likely to hinder as help the necessary reform process is that such aid would inevitably be provided to the Union government, whereas prospects for genuine reform are clearly much better in the Republics. One of the sobering lessons of all U.S. experience with foreign aid from the Marshall Plan to current aid to developing countries is that government-to-government aid strengthens the central government at the expense of the periphery. Hence, notwithstanding the 9-plus-1 Union Treaty, foreign aid to the central Soviet government is bound to strengthen its hand in dealing with the Republics, thereby militating against genuine reform.

One version of the argument for large-scale aid that will probably surface in the coming months focuses on its potentially appealing role in providing a "stabilization reserve" to underwrite convertibility of the ruble. This, too, is flawed. If and as monetary and fiscal balance is attained in the Soviet Union, convertibility with a floating exchange rate can be established with only minimal hard currency reserves. If this balance is not attained, the ensuing run on the stabilization reserve would rapidly exhaust it, thereby aborting convertibility.

With appropriate reform measures, aid will not be needed. Without it, aid will be wasted. Large-scale concessional aid to the Soviet Union is an idea that should be interred before it is revived. It is neither something that the West should promise, nor that those who seek genuine reform in the Soviet Union should be encouraged to expect.

5. Aiding Russia and Ukraine[6]

Although Presidents Clinton and Mitterand and former President Nixon agree on the importance of foreign assistance to Russia, neither they nor other advocates have been specific about how much or what types of aid are appropriate. To the limited extent that specifics have been addressed, doubts are warranted about their feasibility or merit.

In addressing the aid question, several considerations are salient.

First, prior Western aid has elicited mixed, but mainly unfavorable, reactions within Russia. Criticisms, by supporters as well as opponents of Boris Yeltsin, have focused on both the small amounts (far below the $24 billion promised by the G-7 a year ago), as well as the added debt burden this aid has imposed on the already beleaguered Russian economy. Moreover, Western aid to Russia has elicited reactions in Ukraine that are even more unfavorable than those in Russia itself. While Russians view Western aid to date as niggardly, Ukrainians view it invidiously because of what they see as the total neglect of Ukraine's own needs and interests.

Second, future aid from the West should be cognizant of the Hippocratic precept to do no harm (". . . abstain from whatever is deleterious"). In economies like those of Russia and Ukraine that are trying to become more marketized and are beginning to generate and respond to market price signals, foreign subsidies provided through government-to-government aid channels may nullify those signals, thereby retarding rather than advancing marketization.

Finally, aid should be *purposeful rather than personal*: it should seek to advance purposes and policies linked to the fundamentals of transforming the economies

---

[6]A slightly abbreviated version of this essay was published under the title "An Aid Package for Russia—Beyond Clinton's" by the *Wall Street Journal* on April 16, 1993. Reprinted by permission of The Wall Street Journal, © 1993 Dow Jones & Company, Inc. All Rights Reserved Worldwide.

and societies of Russia and Ukraine. While President Yeltsin is eminently deserving of encouragement and support, foreign aid policies should not be so narrowly or personally conceived that their rationale lapses if the Yeltsin government proves to be transitory.

A four-part foreign assistance package, that comports with these considerations, would consist of: (1) debt relief through rescheduling and cancellation of some foreign debt, and swapping some of the remaining debt for equities in state enterprises undergoing privatization; (2) stimulating foreign direct investment in Russia and Ukraine by galvanizing the presently available OPIC investment insurance program, as well as by providing a stimulus to increase private, commercial insurance; (3) establishing a "market stabilizing mechanism" for global arms sales to assure Russia and Ukraine a "reasonable" share of the global arms market; and (4) supplementing the $800 million already appropriated for the dismantling of nuclear weapons with additional funds for these and related purposes.

1. Restructuring and Swapping Foreign Debt

Russia, Ukraine, and six other republics agreed, upon dissolution of the Soviet Union at the end of 1991, to assume "joint and several" responsibility for servicing the entire Soviet external debt, much of which was accumulated preceding and during Mikhail Gorbachev's 1985–1991 tenure. This debt, together with the additional debt incurred in 1992 and 1993, currently is between $75–80 billion. Russia is the only republic that has attempted to meet this extremely onerous servicing obligation. During the next three years, from 1993–1995, the annual burden represented by servicing long-term, hard-currency debt alone will be between $10–14 billion, thereby preempting between one-third and one-half of Russia's annual hard currency foreign exchange earnings.

Two measures can contribute significantly to easing this burden. The first would have the Western creditors (Germany, Italy, and the other West European countries are collectively owed 70 percent of the total, the U.S. only 5 percent) to forgive all or most of the debt incurred before the formal dissolution of the Soviet Union on January 1, 1992. Most of the creditors' banking institutions have already built up loss reserves in anticipation of this prospect, so the financial impact would be modest. Moreover, by linking the debt cutoff to the historic date of the Soviet Union's dissolution, debt forgiveness would avoid a precedent that other debtor countries might invoke in an effort to obtain equal concessions for themselves.

The second measure is to swap some of the remaining sovereign debt for equities in state enterprises undergoing privatization in Russia and Ukraine. Under the Russian privatization law adopted last year, 35,000 state enterprises are to be privatized over the next three years. The process, which is currently underway, calls for 25 percent of the shares to be given to enterprise workers and managers, 30–35 percent to be auctioned to Russia's 150 million citizens in exchange for ruble vouchers already distributed to them, and the remaining shares to be retained by the state. If some of these government-held shares were swapped for debt liabilities, the economic burden of meeting the fixed servicing obligations of debt would be replaced by more flexible servicing obligations that depend instead on the economic performance of equities. Moreover, foreign creditors who acquire these assets will have incentives to enhance their stakes by adding management skills, technology, and improved access to Western markets, as well as by new investment. As the value of the existing debt declines on the secondary debt market, creditors' incentives to engage in such swaps will increase. (Significantly, medium-term Soviet debt that carried a 20 percent discount in the fall of 1992, currently carries a 50 percent discount!)

2. Encouraging Foreign Investment by Expanding Risk Insurance

The United States already has a modest program to encourage foreign investment in Russia and Ukraine by providing subsidized insurance against investors' exposure to political risks of expropriation or violence. This insurance is written by a government agency—the Overseas Private Investment Corporation—for a premium that is less than half the cost of roughly comparable political risk insurance that is sometimes available in the commercial insurance market.

To date, OPIC has approved insurance applications for only seven investments with a face value of $121 million for Russia and none for Ukraine, from an applications pool of 256 for Russia with a face value of $22 billion, and 39 for Ukraine with a face value of $1.7 billion. The limited scale of these approvals is due to many factors, including especially OPIC's understandable reluctance to increase the risks that American taxpayers would be exposed to if turmoil ensued in Russia or Ukraine and compensation to insured investors were required.

However, foreign aid directed toward encouraging private investment is a high-leverage form of aid for furthering market-oriented economic reform. Toward this end, foreign investment in Russia and Ukraine can be boosted in two ways: first, by galvanizing OPIC's existing activities—(for example, by removing the present $200 million limit that applies to insurance for any single company's investment), and second, by providing incentives to the private commercial insurance market—for example, by allowing a tax credit of, say, 50 percent of the premia received from issuance of political risk insurance to U.S. investors in Russia and Ukraine.

3. Assuring Russia and Ukraine a Reasonable Share of the World Arms Market

International weapons sales accounted in the last half of the 1980s for 20 percent of the former Soviet Union's export earnings, compared to about 4 percent for the U.S. To be sure, we have a general interest in both damping down the arms market and in drastic downsizing of Russian and Ukrainian military industry. Reductions of over 60 percent in Russia's defense procurement spending are accomplishing this downsizing. However, we should also acknowledge that Russia and Ukraine have a critical need for hard currency exports, and their comparative advantage for realizing them lies in arms sales.

Provided that exports of potentially destabilizing weapons—like submarines, cruise missiles, or advanced sea and land mines—are controlled, the United States and the other principal weapons exporters (France, Britain, China, and Germany) should establish a cartel-like stabilizing mechanism for the conventional arms market that would envisage for Russia and Ukraine an appreciable share (say, 20 percent) of the $35 billion annual weapons market.

4. Dismantling Nuclear Weapons and Retrofitting Nuclear Reactors

In 1992, the U.S. provided $800 million of Defense Department appropriations for dismantling tactical nuclear weapons in Russia and Ukraine. Less than 5 percent of these funds have been expended thus far, due to logistic, contracting and organizational delays on both the U.S. and Russian sides. In addition to expediting the effective use and expenditure of these funds, the U.S. should adopt a proposal by Robert Ellsworth to expand this effort. This proposal would increase the $800 million fund to assist in further weapons dismantling, as well as in retrofitting with radiation-containment structures the several dozen Chernobyl-type nuclear reactors located in Russia, Ukraine, and other former Soviet states, and dismantling the 300 power reactors on Russian nuclear submarines that are to be decommissioned under existing arms control agreements.

Economic reform and political transformation in Russia and Ukraine inevitably involve military issues, like arms sales and weapons dismantling, because of the distorted gigantism of the military sectors inherited from the Soviet economy. Consequently, an effective economic aid package should include components that address these matters, as well as furthering purposes like debt abatement and foreign investment promotion, that Presidents Yeltsin and Kravchuk endorse, but that transcend their personal tenures. Finally, an effective aid package should be realistic and feasible, and not promise more than can be delivered, as Western aid has sometimes done in recent years.

6. Independence for Ukraine and Russia[7]

On December 1st, the Ukrainian electorate will probably endorse by a large majority a democratic referendum establishing the Republic's sovereign independence. Notwithstanding the pending referendum, as well as Ukraine's decision two weeks ago to sign a broad, although vague, economic cooperation treaty with nine other republics of the former Soviet Union (FSU), a central question remains unresolved: Precisely what economic relationships should be sought between the two principal republics, Russia and Ukraine, which together comprise 70 percent of the FSU's population and 80 percent of its gross product? The options range from sharp separation to close economic linkage between the two republics.

In sorting out the advantages and disadvantages of each option, as well as considering whether the United States should favor or deliberately avoid favoring either one, there is merit in reflecting on what would be in the best economic interests of Russia and Ukraine. Contrary to much of the conventional wisdom, separate and sovereign economic status would be economically preferable for both republics.

Prospects for economic improvement in both Russia and Ukraine will be enhanced by rapid and inclusive marketization of their command economies. In turn, marketization depends on the simultaneous, or at least contemporaneous, implementation of six essential reforms. And implementation of these reforms is more likely if the two republics have economically separate status.

The essential reforms include: monetary reform to ensure control of the money supply and credit; fiscal control to assure budgetary balance and to limit monetization of a budget deficit if one occurs; price and wage deregulation to

---

[7]A slightly abbreviated version of this essay was published by the *Wall Street Journal* on November 29, 1991. Reprinted by permission of The Wall Street Journal, © 1991 Dow Jones & Company, Inc. All Rights Reserved Worldwide.

link prices and wages to costs and productivity, respectively; privatization, legal protection of property rights, and the breakup of state monopolies (including defense industry); a social "safety net" to protect those who may become unemployed; and currency convertibility to link the transforming economies to the world economy and to competition in international markets.

The first two elements (monetary reform and fiscal control) and the fifth (the social safety net) create the broad macroeconomic environment that enables the incentive mechanisms of the other three to move resources toward more efficient and growth-promoting uses.

The proposals that Boris Yeltsin has recently induced the Russian parliament to accept include most of these essential elements. The challenge and uncertainty lie in their implementation.

Separate economic status for the Russian and Ukrainian republics will improve prospects for implementation. And the several components of marketizaton will be advanced by this status.

With respect to implementation, less bureaucratic interference and fewer delays can be expected if the republics are economically separate rather than joined. One reason relates to the diseconomies of scale in large bureaucracies: a bureaucracy that covers both Ukraine and Russia will simply be bigger, more cumbersome, and less flexible than a smaller one. A second reason is that marketization will be able to proceed more rapidly if it is separate from the ethnic and nationalistic overtones and second-guessing that is likely to ensue if Russia and Ukraine are closely linked.

Furthermore, separate and independent republics would provide greater room for experimentation with different modalities of reform. For example, there isn't a single demonstrably preferable mode of privatization. It should be possible to experiment with several different modes if the units are smaller rather than the enormous one that would result from closely linking Russia and Ukraine.

With respect to the specific components of marketization, *fiscal and monetary control* is probably easier to accomplish if the implementing units are smaller.

Price and wage deregulation will be neither more nor less difficult if the two republics are separate or joined. As noted above, *property rights and privatization* are areas for active experimentation with alternative modes, and this should be easier to do in small rather than large political jurisdictions. The *social safety net* may be one area in which a larger economic entity rather than two smaller ones is preferable because it would provide more opportunity for spreading risk (analogous to hedging by portfolio diversification). In any event, however, Ukraine should be large enough on this count, even if it is only a third of the size of the Russian republic.

Finally, with respect to *currency convertibility*, prospects for moving in this direction are better if the two republics are separate, each with its own floating but convertible rate. Ukraine can probably aspire to achieve this more quickly than either Russia alone, or the two republics together.

To be sure, numerous economic arguments have been advanced against separation and in favor of close linkage between Ukraine and Russia. But these arguments are unconvincing.

One argument is that the Russian and Ukrainian republics should be closely joined because they are economically interdependent as a result of decades of monopolistic industries located in each area. The short rebuttal to this is simply free trade between the republics. This, combined with rapid movement toward price and wage deregulation within both republics, will be necessary to uncover the realities of comparative costs that have been obscured by command prices.

Second is the argument that it will be more difficult to divide the $80 billion of external Soviet debt if the republics are entirely separate from one another. But this misses the point: The real burden of debt servicing will inevitably be the subject of dispute and negotiation among different parts of the FSU, whether the republics are integrated or separate.

A third argument is that convertibility will be harder to establish if there are two separate Ukrainian and Russian currencies. This argument is also flawed. If both currencies are convertible, convertibility between them is established, q.e.d.

If, on the other hand, only one is convertible, then at least the process of reform has advanced in that singular case.

In sum, two are better than one! If the United States chooses, for political reasons, not to take a position in favor of separation of the two republics, it should, for economic reasons, at least avoid favoring a close linkage between them.

7. Some Hopeful Signs Midst the Commonwealth's Economic Travails[8]

With the remarkably swift establishment of the Commonwealth of Independent States (CIS) on December 21, 1991, the leaders of its member republics should be able to turn their attention from politics to economics. Expecting the worst, they may have reason to be encouraged by what they find. While there is no doubt that the economies of the republics—especially Russia and Ukraine—are in trouble, considerable doubt is warranted that the actual trouble is as deep and dire as asserted by numerous recent alarmist pronouncements.

These forebodings have included forecasts by Eduard Shevardnadze that the gross national product will decrease to half its 1990 level, by Secretary Baker that we may be seeing "the economy collapse with no bottom in sight," and by Pravda that "total pauperization of the people and final collapse of the monetary system" impend.

Official Soviet data from the State Statistics Commission (GOSKOMSTAT) and from published CIA figures, which underlie the foregoing prophesies, are also profoundly pessimistic. These sources estimate a fall in GNP of 15 percent in 1991 and forecast a further decline in 1992 of 20 percent or more.

These gloomy assessments result, in considerable part, from the shortcomings of the official statistics, as well as from observation of the bare shelves in state stores. But these are imperfect and unreliable indicators because transactions are increasingly taking place outside the official distribution channels. Consequently, the official statistics are of limited help in tracking the economic

---

[8]A slightly abbreviated version of this essay was published under the title "Reasons for Economic Optimism in Ex-U.S.S.R." by the *Wall Street Journal* on January 3, 1992. Reprinted by permission of The Wall Street Journal, © 1992 Dow Jones & Company, Inc. All Rights Reserved Worldwide.

activity that is occurring in the wake of erosion of the superstructure of the former command system, and appearance of the early signs of an emerging market economy.

One of the striking ironies in the current situation is that the official data, which in the past substantially and perennially *overestimated* the size and performance of the Soviet economy, are probably now substantially *underestimating* the economic condition of the principal republic economies. Moreover, the previous overestimates have contributed to exaggerated estimates of how far the economy must have fallen to get to its present position. Not having been where it was believed to be, the economy appears to have fallen farther to arrive where it presently is!

For marketization to proceed, one of the quintessential requisites is removal of the bureaucratic command structure that formerly prevented, and more recently has distorted, the operation of market forces. Much of the current economic disarray reflects this process—a process that can be likened to what Joseph Schumpeter characterized, in another context, as "creative destruction." As the process proceeds, economic activity has gravitated away from the former official economy and toward the "second" or "underground" economy. What were initially "leakages" from the official economy have become streams that eventually will become a flood to the former second economy as this becomes the real economy of the republics. Marketization in the CIS republics can be plausibly viewed as a process in which the gray and black markets become open and official, thus displacing the former non-market command system.

Evidence of this process is inevitably incomplete and anecdotal, but nonetheless significant.

As the previously existing long-haul distribution systems have become sundered, localized economic activities and new channels of production and distribution have begun to appear. More than 400 commodity exchanges have developed to facilitate such local activities, often through barter transactions. As David Brooks has observed (*Wall Street Journal*, December 10, 1991), "entrepreneurs are sprouting up like weeds." There are also frequent instances where enterprises—

both military and non-military ones—are devoting overtime shifts to producing output for payment in kind to employees and for barter exchange on the gray or black markets. And there are indications that some of the principal republics' external trade—imports as well as exports—is taking place outside official reporting channels.

Most if not all of these types and signs of burgeoning economic activity are omitted from the official data collection.

This is not to say that the economic picture is rosy in Russia, Ukraine, and the other republics of the CIS, especially in certain of their key urban centers: The shelves of state stores are bare, prices on the unofficial markets have soared, and the ruble has been debased by enormous expansion of the money supply. Nor does it deny that some forms of external assistance may be of high priority in special circumstances—including assistance to establish more reliable means for measuring economic activity in general and progress in particular. But it does suggest that the repeated assertions and forecasts of unrelieved decline and gloom are exaggerated and unconvincing because they are based on misleadingly incomplete data.

It also suggests that the prospects for success of Boris Yeltsin's initial package of economic reforms—notably, price and wage decontrol combined with fiscal (and, one hopes, monetary) stabilization—may be brighter than is commonly assumed, and that these prospects may be improved by the growth of market-oriented economic activity that is already underway.

8. Limited Optimism Rather Than Boundless Pessimism About the Russian Economy[9]

The current consensus among putative experts places the Russian economy's prospects as somewhere between poor and dismal. But the consensus may be wrong. To be sure, there are legitimate reasons for the prevailing pessimism. However, there are other reasons that lead to more optimism, or at least less pessimism, than the consensus implies.

The principal concerns contributing to the gloomy assessment include: the insufficiency of economic reform measures undertaken by President Boris Yeltsin and Acting Prime Minister Yegor Gaidar, the sharp declines reported in Russian GNP and employment, the sustained and growing budget and "off-budget" deficits, the consequent risk of hyperinflation, and the enormous unresolved problems of converting Russian military industry to civil pursuits.

The insufficiencies of the Yeltsin-Gaidar reforms stand out clearly when compared with what needs to be done. Transforming Russia's command economy into a market-oriented one requires implementation of five essential and mutually reinforcing measures: fiscal and monetary stabilization (a balanced budget and control of the money supply); decontrol of prices and wages; assuring property rights, privatization, demonopolization, and free entry of competing new enterprises; currency convertibility; and a suitable social safety net. The interactions among these measures mean that the effectiveness of any one will be reduced if the others are not in train.

Viewed in this light, the Yeltsin-Gaidar program has indeed been modest. It has concentrated on price and wage decontrol combined with fiscal and monetary

---

[9]This essay was published under the title "Reasons for Hope" by *World Monitor The Christian Science Monitor Monthly* in January 1993.

stabilization efforts. And even these limited efforts have been associated with insufficient implementation by the bureaucracy, as well as backtracking by government in response to resistance and opposition from the so-called "conservative" forces in the Russian parliament. Contrary to its previously announced policy, the government has been obliged to extend large subsidies to unproductive state enterprises, resulting in budget deficits that add to a continually expanding money supply.

The inadequacy of Gaidar's efforts to bring about macroeconomic stabilization is reflected by the mounting Russian budget deficit, which reached over 120 billion rubles during the first five months of 1992. For 1992 as a whole, the deficit will be about 17 percent of the Russian GNP. (In comparison, the swollen U.S. federal government budget deficit is less than 6 percent of U.S. GNP). Worries about the possibility of hyperinflation are also evoked by the enormous increase of over two trillion rubles in inter-enterprise credits.

Moreover, with regard to another important dimension of reform, progress toward privatization and demonopolization of state industry has been virtually nil.

Still another factor on the downside are the serious declines in Russian GNP, reported as 17 percent in 1991, with a drop of more than 25 percent estimated for 1992.

Thus, the reasons that underlie the pessimistic consensus are numerous and serious. But they tell only part of the story. There are other parts that are more encouraging.

First, consider the statistics purporting to show a sharp decline in Soviet GNP. It is ironic that the official data, which in the past perennially *overestimated* the size and performance of the then-Soviet economy, are now almost certainly *underestimating* the economic condition of Russia and the other principal republics. Indeed, the previous overestimates have contributed to exaggerated estimates of how far the economy has fallen to get to its present position. Not having been where it was believed to be, the economy appears to have fallen farther to arrive where it now is!

The official data on Russian real output are in error because they fail to cover much new economic activity—especially output of food and consumer goods—that deliberately evades official data collection agencies. One reason for the systematic underreporting is the desire of producers, especially new entrepreneurs, to avoid high government taxes—notably the 28 percent value-added tax, and the 32 percent business profits tax. As a result, prices in the flourishing black or gray markets are sometimes lower than those in Russian state stores!

Another reason for the systematic underreporting of real output is the use of equipment and input supplies by state enterprises for "moonlighting" production, which finds its way into "non-institutional" (i.e., "black" or "gray") markets, including export markets. This results in under-invoicing or non-invoicing of some exports, and the accumulation of hard currency deposits that are held abroad. The latter represents a flight of capital whose repatriation to Russia will depend on creating an environment that makes its use in the domestic economy profitable.

Still another source of underreporting is the disruption of the previously existing long-haul distribution systems of the Soviet economy. As a result, localized economic activities and new channels of production and distribution have begun to appear. Hundreds of commodity exchanges have developed to facilitate such local transactions, often through barter, and sometimes involving the "moonlighted" production of both military and non-military state enterprises.

Furthermore, to the extent that declines in real output have actually occurred, they are a misleading indicator of consumer well-being. Much of the declines represent reductions of military output, as well as output of producers' durable goods and heavy metallurgical industry, rather than of consumer goods.

Next, consider the budget deficit and the expanded monetary stock. This problem has probably also been exaggerated. For example, the enormous increase in inter-enterprise ruble credits represents a nominal increase in the monetary stock whose turnover velocity is low. Although there is a possibility that part of these huge "accounts receivable" will be monetized, this is likely to take place slowly and to have only a limited effect on the risk of hyperinflation.

Turning to the vital issue of property rights, privatization, and demonopolization of state industry, it is true that progress has been disappointingly slow. Nevertheless, the new privatization law promulgated at the end of June 1992 is encouraging. The law is intended to privatize 70 percent of all industrial assets and a higher proportion of total Russian manufacturing value-added, according to the chief economist of the powerful Association of Industrialists and Entrepreneurs, Yevgeny Yasin. The government's declared aim is to accomplish this goal within three years, although Yasin indicated to me in June his belief that it would (and should!) take longer. The law provides for privatization of state enterprises through various forms of stock distribution. These include an initial gift of 25 percent of the shares to enterprise workers, as well as sale of another 5 percent to managers at "book value" (an elusive standard because of the absence of a price system for assessing book value and depreciation). The remaining shares are to be available for purchase by workers and managers, as well as by Russian citizens using vouchers distributed to them. These shares will also be available for bidding by foreign investors at the enterprise auctions planned in the coming months.

It remains to be seen how well the privatization plan will be implemented. Ironically, the fact that it has already been criticized from all sides of the political and ideological spectrum is probably an encouraging sign of the plan's merit. For example, the staunchly pro-market, free enterprise advocates on what in Russia is viewed as the liberal "left," criticize the plan because its targets are too low, its pace too slow, and its bureaucratic complexity too Byzantine. These critics include Larisa Piyasheva, Vasilii Selunin, and Boris Pinsker, among others. The plan is also criticized from the conservative "right"—for example by Arkadi Volsky and Yasin on behalf of the Association of Industrialists and Entrepreneurs—on the grounds that it is too ambitious, too rapid, and too rigid.

It is important to note that the intense differences among these competing views are associated with a key characteristic that should allow compromises to be worked out. This characteristic relates to the continuity, rather than discontinuity, of the underlying issues separating the reforming activists from the bureaucracy, as well as from the enterprise managers and workers. These issues include not only the pace and character of privatization, but also the other dimensions of systemic transformation—notably, monetary and fiscal stabilization, and price decontrol. All of these elements can be implemented more or less fully, and more or less rapidly. *They are inherently "more-or-less" in nature, rather than binary "all-or-nothing."* Political compromises are more likely than would be the case if the contending issues were binary because binary issues provide less of an opportunity for "splitting the difference" between contesting parties.

One important issue for the success of reform efforts, not only in Russia but in the other republics as well, involves the resumption of trade among the republics. The special importance of such trade derives from an unfortunate legacy of the Soviet command economy that established monopolies for production of particular equipment or other products in one or another republic. The aim of this misguided effort was to achieve economies of large-scale production. The actual result was to create critical interdependencies among the different republics and regions of the Soviet economy.

However, since dissolution of the Soviet Union in January 1992, trade channels among the republics have been disrupted, with seriously adverse repercussions for the separate economies, particularly those of Russia and Ukraine. For example, the Ukrainian economy had previously relied on crude oil, textiles, and metallurgical products from Russia, while the Russian economy imported food and some finished machinery and electronic products from Ukraine. These prior trade channels have been disrupted by the breakup of the Union. Prospects for removal of trade barriers among the republics are unclear, although the benefits from such openings would be enormous.

Here again there are signs that progress can be made through reasonable compromises. One encouraging indicator that the trade impasse can be resolved is the recent compromise between Russia and Ukraine over the highly explosive issue of responsibility for the Black Sea fleet, which both republics had previously claimed. In early August 1992, Russia and Ukraine agreed to share responsibility for command and operations of the fleet over the next three and a half years—a compromise that also augurs well for compromises on the trade issue.

Finally, the Russian economy's prospects are inevitably complicated by the enormously swollen scale of military industry in the economy. At least 25 percent of Soviet GNP was directly or indirectly accounted for by military industry, as well as a much larger fraction of high technology industry, and top quality human and physical inputs. How and how rapidly these resources are to be diverted to production for the civil sector will have serious consequences for the marketization and development of the Russian economy as a whole.

On the positive side, there is widespread consensus, as well as resignation, among managers of military industry on the necessity for deep reductions in military production, and conversion of industrial assets toward civilian production. The new privatization law, which will encompass some, though not all, parts of the Russian military industrial complex, is another encouraging sign. There are also innumerable examples and anecdotes about new joint ventures between elements of Russian military industry and foreign investors. For instance, one particular military enterprise that produced top quality guidance systems for the most advanced Soviet ICBM systems has both equipment and skilled personnel capable of producing top quality surgical equipment for eventual export on world markets. Despite such anecdotes, very little has been accomplished in military conversion.

Although most military industry assets will have to be redeployed or scrapped, the Russian economy will still probably maintain an appreciable military industrial base to support the future Russian military establishment, as well as to export on international arms markets. For effective conversion to proceed, what is needed is an opening and loosening of the government strictures that still confine military enterprises. The large assets they control should be available for redeployment to civilian uses by both new Russian entrepreneurs acting alone or in concert with foreign joint ventures.

In sum, there are positive and encouraging signs, as well as negative and discouraging ones. This is not a case where the glass is half full, nor is it one in which the glass is entirely empty. The Russian economy could encounter hyperinflation. The polity might experience a sharp swing to the right. And fragmentation and civil strife might occur within or among the republics of the Commonwealth of Independent States. On the other hand, reforms may proceed. Compromises may be made. And marketization may gain momentum and succeed.

Policies followed by the United States and the other G-7 governments can be of some help in contributing to a more favorable outcome, but this help will inevitably be limited. Though the symbolic as well as material importance of the West's $24 billion aid package should not be underestimated, the principal emphasis of Western efforts should be focused on facilitating private investment and trade: specifically, on accelerating Russian access to both the international capital market—perhaps with the assistance of government-financed investment guarantees—and to goods markets through the extension of most-favored-nation access by the U.S. and European Community markets.

But the decisive role will not be played by the West. It will be played by the Russians, and they know it. In the midst of all the heated controversies in Russian political and economic circles, that recognition itself is an encouraging sign—a sign that warrants moderate optimism rather than boundless pessimism about the Russian economy's prospects.

9. Sweepstakes Capitalism[10]

Privatization is the top priority on the agenda of the reforming economies of
Poland, Czechoslovakia, and Hungary. And there is nearly unanimous
agreement among the political leaders of these countries, as well as their
technical advisors, that a drastic shift of ownership of state enterprises from
government to private hands is essential if these economies are to become
competitive, market-based systems. (Privatization is no less essential in the
Soviet Union, but its endorsement is much more ambiguous among the Soviet
leadership in Moscow than in several of the Soviet Republics, especially the
Russian Republic.)

Despite widespread acceptance of the goal, there remains intense disagreement
about the methods, mechanisms, and speed of accomplishing it. Underlying the
disagreement is a series of issues and obstacles, some spurious and some serious.
The obstacles can be surmounted by a process that is simple, understandable and
practicable; namely, privatizing by randomizing!

Because of the disagreements about appropriate methods and speed,
privatization has proceeded at a snail's pace. In Poland, less than 5 percent of the
state enterprises (fewer than 150 out of an estimated 3100 state enterprises) have
been privatized—only 7 in 1990—and about 75 percent of total industrial
capacity remains in government hands. Moreover, much of the remaining 25
percent has resulted from the start-up of new ventures, rather than the
privatization and breakup of the large, established state enterprises. (Recently,
Poland proposed a complex plan to privatize an additional 400 state enterprises
by placing them in the hands of 20 investment funds, and providing to each of
Poland's 27 million adult citizens one share in each fund. The plan remains to be
debated and approved by the Polish parliament.) In the other East European

---

[10]A slightly abbreviated version of this essay was published by the *Wall Street Journal* on July 12,
1991. Reprinted by permission of The Wall Street Journal, © 1991 Dow Jones & Company, Inc. All
Rights Reserved Worldwide.

countries, progress has been even slower and still more limited. In the Soviet Union, it has been negligible.

Government officials responsible for privatization in Eastern Europe extenuate their record by noting that Margaret Thatcher succeeded in denationalizing only a dozen state enterprises during her 10 years as Prime Minister! But the comparison is inapt. The British effort sought to bring the previously nationalized airline, railway, and telecommunications companies toward a point of profitability before selling shares to the public on the London exchange—a goal that is neither necessary nor practicable for existing state enterprises in Eastern Europe. Furthermore, despite the nationalization efforts of Britain's previous Labor governments, the bulk of Britain's industrial capacity—probably more than 80 percent—was still privately owned when the Thatcher program of privatization began in the early 1980s. Finally, the British example is not one that Eastern Europe should follow for yet another reason: the British government has retained a so-called "golden share" in several of the denationalized industries enabling the government to exercise an ultimate veto if it chose to do so, even *after* privatization.

Another objection raised against privatization in Eastern Europe is the lack of a suitable basis for valuation of the state enterprises to be privatized. It is argued that, until market forces can determine prices of output, as well as the costs of labor and other key inputs, enterprise profitability cannot be evaluated, and thus suitable values cannot be established for privatizing enterprise assets.

This objection is spurious. It arises from a misconception about the meaning of privatization. Privatization is simply the vesting or assignment of property rights in private hands. Market valuation can facilitate the vesting process, but it is not essential. What is essential is an effective means for shifting ownership from state to private hands in the interests of improving incentives, efficiency, and productivity.

Another objection to rapid privatization is that many of the large holders of liquid capital in the Eastern European countries (and in the Soviet Union as well), are said to have previously been members of the Communist *nomenklatura*, black marketeers, or "mafiosi." Consequently, their prospective acquisition of state enterprises—through, say, an auction sale—would be politically unacceptable and socially inequitable.

Although there are legitimate grounds for this concern, they don't invalidate the case for privatization. To repeat, privatization requires neither liquid capital nor market valuation. Instead, it requires a mechanism for divesting ownership from the state and vesting it in private hands.

One method that has been proposed for accomplishing rapid privatization is to issue vouchers or coupons representing ownership shares to specified groups of enterprise "insiders" and "outsiders": for example, 20 percent to workers and management as enterprise "insiders," 15–20 percent to state banks that are themselves being privatized, 20 percent to pension funds, 30 percent to new mutual funds, and the remainder to be retained by government for later sales as a market for stock shares develops. The "black box" character of these or other percentage assignments has led to criticism and resistance to this proposal on the grounds that it is both "technocratic" and "inequitable": "technocratic" because the choice of percentages is viewed as mechanistic and unintelligible; and "inequitable" because of suspicion that the small number of potentially profitable enterprises among the larger number of potential losers will be distributed to favored groups operating behind a veil of bureaucratic decisionmaking.

By contrast, randomization provides a method of accomplishing rapid privatization, while avoiding these pitfalls.

"Privatizing by randomizing" means that all ownership shares of state enterprises would be distributed to the general public—except for, say, a 20 percent "inducement" package for each enterprise's own employees and management to enlist their support—by means of a national lottery. *Ex ante*, each citizen would have an equal chance of receiving shares of prospectively profitable enterprises, as well as of non-viable ones. The "equitableness" of the randomization process derives from the equality of each citizen's initial chance of receiving a valuable or a valueless asset. Randomization has the further advantage of simplicity and intelligibility. If administered honestly, randomization is a means of speeding privatization—of getting the large state enterprises into private hands so that market forces can move them toward more efficient use, toward breakup into smaller entities, or to liquidation. As privatization proceeds, enterprise managers will become responsible to private shareholders who may choose new management, or sell their shares to other buyers, or decide to sell off parts of the large industrial enterprises to new and smaller enterprises.

To be sure, privatization is only one step—albeit a tremendous one—toward efficiency. And it must be underwritten by an appropriate legal code that protects property rights and provides a means for resolving disputes about them.

Nevertheless, accelerating privatization by randomization through a national lottery can jump-start an essential but presently stalled part of the process of transforming centrally planned economies into genuine market systems.

10. Swapping Debt for Equity in Russia[11]

One of the major obstacles to improving performance of the Russian economy is the heavy burden of servicing $70 billion of inherited Soviet sovereign debt, much of it accumulated during Mikhail Gorbachev's tenure from 1985 through 1991. The burden can be measurably eased by giving foreign creditors the option of swapping existing debt for equity shares in Russia's privatizing state enterprises. As a result, not only can the debt burden be eased, but a boost can be given to privatization and foreign investment, as well.

One month prior to the Soviet Union's formal dissolution on January 1, 1992, Russia, Ukraine, and six other republics of the former Soviet Union agreed to assume "joint and several" responsibility for servicing the entire Soviet external debt. The understanding was that Russia would provide 60 percent of the annual servicing payments, although in principle each of the signatories assumed full liability if other signatories failed to meet their shared obligations. In fact, Russia is the only republic currently in compliance with these obligations.

The large annual servicing burden, currently $9 billion, represents 30 percent of Russia's annual foreign exchange earnings, and about one half of the annual net foreign loans and grants announced by the G-7, but not yet fully disbursed to the Commonwealth republics. In effect, the G-7 donors, including the International Monetary Fund and World Bank, are paying with one hand, while withdrawing with the other—in the process, adding to the debt burden that Russia and the other republics will face in the future.

This smoke-and-mirrors artifice recalls the Latin American debt predicament in the 1980s, which gave rise to the Baker Plan in 1985 and the Brady Plan in 1989. These plans called for debt-equity swaps to ease the heavy debt burden and to

---

[11]A slightly abbreviated version of this essay was published under the title "Latin-Style Swaps for Russia" by the *Wall Street Journal* on November 19, 1992. Reprinted by permission of The Wall Street Journal, © 1992 Dow Jones & Company, Inc. All Rights Reserved Worldwide.

promote privatization reform in Latin America, especially in Brazil, Mexico, and Argentina. (Actually, both the Baker and Brady Plans were foreshadowed by earlier proposals of Kiichi Miyazawa, then Japan's finance minister and currently its prime minister). The ensuing swaps played a modest, but significant, role in converting Latin America's debt "crisis" into a more manageable, albeit still serious, financial problem. Moreover, some of the large Latin American creditors, such as Citicorp, that swapped debt for equities in the late 1980s realized very large profits from the subsequent resale of their equity acquisitions.

In Russia, the swap option could conceivably play a still more significant role than it did in Latin America. The privatization plans of Boris Yeltsin's government envisage conversion of a huge number of state enterprises into privatized, joint-stock companies. The magnitude and range of equities that can be put in play for debt conversion in Russia dwarfs what was available in Latin America. Although many of these enterprises have dubious prospects for survival, others are likely to be highly valuable, because they possess valuable assets in such fields as fiber optics, electronics, propulsion, and metallurgy. Consequently, Russia's creditors, or their surrogates, should have a much wider and potentially more attractive range of opportunities and choices than were available in the Latin American precedent.

Russia's privatization law, promulgated in July 1992, calls for conversion of 70 percent of the assets of over 35,000 state enterprises to joint-stock ownership, over three years. To be sure, Russia's Union of Industrialists and Entrepreneurs, whose membership includes most of the larger enterprises, and its head, Arkady Volsky, argue that the privatization process should be reduced in scope and implemented more slowly than the law envisages. In any event, a massive privatization process will ensue even if the Volsky group manages to moderate its pace and scale.

The initial privatization *tranche* planned for December 1992 will market some 7,000 state enterprises, through several different channels: gifts of shares to enterprise workers (20 percent of the total shares) and managers (another 5 percent); privatization vouchers distributed to each of Russia's 150 million citizens, with a nominal face value of 10,000 rubles per voucher, accounting for

30 percent of the enterprises' shares; and the remaining 45 percent initially to be retained by government and available for subsequent sale.

These residual shares held by government provide the means for implementing a swap of some of the outstanding sovereign debt shouldered by Russia. Moreover, further down the road, the debt swaps can draw on a corresponding proportion of the more than 28,000 state enterprises that remain to be privatized in later phases of the process.

From the standpoint of Russia's foreign creditors (the principal one is Germany), the key question concerns the worth of the enterprises' stock. The answer is something between a puzzle and an enigma. In establishing the face value of each voucher at 10,000 rubles, the economists on Acting Prime Minister Yegor Gaidar's team based their estimates on the book-value of the 7,000 enterprises' assets recalculated in 1991 ruble prices. At these prices, the resulting 1.5 trillion ruble estimate represented perhaps $10 billion. Actually, the true market value of these assets is impossible to infer from these estimates both because the 1991 ruble prices were themselves not free market prices, and because even updated book values are imperfect indicators of the market values of the enterprises' assets.

In any event, the potential value of the assets that might be involved in debt swaps—including land, structures, equipment, and the human capital associated with the enterprises—may be large enough to make an appreciable contribution to easing the burden imposed by the existing foreign debt. To implement the debt-for-equity idea requires that two domains of Russian policymaking that have hitherto proceeded along more or less separate paths, should be closely linked—namely, privatization under Deputy Prime Minister Anatoli Chubais, and foreign debt servicing and rescheduling under Deputy Prime Minister Alexander Shokhin. Both foreign creditors and the Russian economy can thereby benefit.

Creditors can benefit from the opportunity of exchanging assets whose value will probably depreciate for assets that have a potential for appreciation. To be sure, the creditors will face a challenge of sifting through a large volume of diverse equities whose future market value may be quite uncertain. But the creditors also know that the value of the sovereign Russian debt that they hold is itself highly uncertain. This debt currently trades at a 20 percent discount in the secondary debt market—and this discount is bound to increase as Russian efforts to reschedule the debt proceed, and as servicing payments predictably lag. Consequently, equity swaps may be relatively attractive despite the uncertainty of the equities' value, because the alternative of retaining debt will become decreasingly attractive to creditors.

The Russian economy can also realize significant benefits through the swaps. The economy's servicing burden will be eased by exchanging assets carrying fixed obligations for those whose servicing depends on asset performance. Moreover, foreign creditors who acquire these assets, or their subsequent purchasers, will have incentives to enhance their stakes by adding management skills, technology, improved access to Western markets, and new investment, thereby contributing to the Russian economy's development and reform.

II. The Changing International Economic Environment

11. Military Power, Economic Power, and a Less Disorderly World[12]

Prior to Desert Storm and Desert Shield, it had become fashionable in some intellectual and political circles, as well as in the media, to predict the receding importance of military power, and its replacement by economic power in the hierarchy of global policy instruments.

Developments in the Middle East since August 1990 have silenced, perhaps only temporarily, the earlier rhetoric about the obsolescence of military power. Nevertheless, while these developments have strikingly demonstrated the importance of military power, the Gulf war also demonstrated an equally important point about the crucial role of economic power.

Economic instruments of power—including capital, technology, goods, and services—are intimately linked with those of military power. And the linkages are often complex, subtle, and significant. Economic power often complements military power, rather than substituting for it, although there are also instances where each can substitute for the other. The converse proposition—that military power often complements economic power—is no less true. (As physicist Nils Bohr once observed, the opposite of a shallow truth is false, while the opposite of a deep truth can also be true.)

In the specific case of the Gulf war, economic power was a vital adjunct of military power. Curtailment of Iraq's access to oil revenues and to imports contributed to weakening its capabilities for resistance. And economic interests and incentives provided important elements in bonding the extraordinary U.S.-led, 29-nation coalition engaged in Desert Shield and Desert Storm. Forgiveness of Egypt's $7 billion military debt to the United States, as well as the promise of

---

[12]A slightly abbreviated version of this essay was published under the title "Money and Might—Policy Handmaidens" by the *Los Angeles Times* on May 6, 1991.

more direct economic support in the future, were important in enlisting and sustaining Egypt's vital role in the coalition. Assurance to Turkey that it would receive offsets to the economic sacrifices it made in embargoing oil deliveries from Iraq played a similarly crucial role in facilitating its participation in the coalition.

Although the Soviet Union's direct participation in the coalition was limited— confined to a couple of naval vessels in the Gulf to help enforce the embargo against Iraq—its political role in supporting the 12 Security Council resolutions was important. To be sure, this role became somewhat tendentious, if not mischievous, in the final stages of the war. Nevertheless, the generally supportive stance of the Union government was valuable, and doubtless was influenced by Soviet interest in avoiding anything that might further impair its access to Western trade, technology, and finance.

In a similar vein, other members of the diverse coalition—notably, Syria, Pakistan, Czechoslovakia, and Poland—were surely influenced by considerations of economic interest and access. In these cases, economic leverage contributed to enhancing military effectiveness. In other instances, the causality runs the other way. A case in point has been Saudi Arabia's steadfast resistance in the war's aftermath to OPEC pressure to reduce oil production and raise oil prices. Thus, the U.S. military effort to protect Saudi security has resulted in economic benefits to the United States, as well as other oil importers.

The closeness, as well as complexity, of the linkages between economic and military power are also exemplified by the anomalous roles of Japan and Germany in the Gulf crisis. Both countries opted to provide funds rather than forces, due to real or alleged political constraints that hindered their deployment of forces abroad. To this extent, economic instruments substituted, although imperfectly, for military ones. However, from the standpoint of the coalition as a whole, the Japanese and German financial commitments—which still remain to be fully implemented—helped to support the coalition by providing economic benefits (or relief from costs) for several of the "frontline" states whose military participation would otherwise have been more problematic.

In the war's murky aftermath, the interplay between economic and military instruments is also crucial. Constructing, protecting, and supplying enclaves for the Kurds has depended on the coordinated use of economic and military measures. If a durable political solution is to be found to the plight of the majority Kurdish and Shi'ite populations of Iraq, the solution will require a combined application of military and economic instruments by countries within and outside the Middle East.

For the United States and other countries to make progress in fashioning a less disorderly world, if not a "new world order," coalitions and collective institutions that prominently involve Third World countries, as well as others, will be of central importance. And economic as well as military instruments will be essential in bringing such coalitions and institutions into being, or in revitalizing existing ones, whether within or outside the United Nations. If this process is to be effective, the economic and military instruments of power will have to be carefully coordinated. They will often turn out to be closely complementary, rather than in opposition, to one another.

12. Why Asia Will Matter More Than Europe[13]

Viewed from a Washington perspective, Europe and the Atlantic generally seem closer, more accessible, and more important than Asia and the Pacific. Deep and abiding linkages of culture, history, politics, and economics underlie this European orientation of much U.S. policymaking and many policymakers. But this perspective is anachronistic. If "economic security" policy is to be at least equal in importance to "national security" policy, as the Clinton Administration intends, and if economic strength in the 1990s is considered no less significant than military strength, as much of the newly conventional thinking on foreign policy asserts, then U.S. policymakers should devote more attention to the Asia Pacific (AP) region in the coming years, even if this means less devoted to Europe.

This change in regional priorities suggests that President Clinton's Departments of State and Commerce, under Secretaries Warren Christopher and Ronald Brown, respectively, and the U.S. Trade Representative Mickey Kantor, should post their best and brightest to work in or on the AP region. Furthermore, federal government agencies should emulate the efforts of many state governments in devoting more of their trade and investment promotion efforts to the AP region, while state governments should continue and reinforce their own efforts as well. And the U.S. Information Agency's Voice of America programming, cultural activities, and foreign leaders' travel grants should place relatively more emphasis on the AP region and AP audiences. Finally, because *economic* security and *national* security policies are likely to be closely related in the AP region, the Defense Secretary, Les Aspin, should be intimately involved in these reorientation efforts.

---

[13]A slightly abbreviated version of this essay was published under the title "Why Asia Pacific Holds the Cards" by the *New York Times* on January 17, 1993. Copyright © 1993 by The New York Times Company. Reprinted by permission.

There are impressive, well-known, but often forgotten reasons that warrant such a shift in the regional emphasis of U.S. policy.

The AP region in the 1990s will encompass the world's most rapidly growing countries. Within this region, China is likely to be the fastest growing economy with an annual growth rate of about 6 percent, while Japan is likely to have the slowest growth in the region (between 2 and 2-1/2 percent annually), except perhaps for that of the Philippines. In between, but probably much closer to China's growth rate than to Japan's will be the other AP economies—Taiwan, Hong Kong (becoming part of China in 1997), Indonesia, Thailand, Singapore, Malaysia, and Korea (assuming that Korea's management of eventual reunification with the North is accomplished peacefully and successfully).

Together the gross national products of the AP economies account for more than 20 percent of the global product—slightly less than the corresponding shares of the United States (23 percent) and the European Community (EC) (28 percent). Within the AP region, China's GNP (which, according to RAND analysis, is about three-times as large as the estimate usually cited by the World Bank and other international agencies) will probably exceed that of Japan before the end of the 1990s. The AP share of the global product will increase appreciably in the coming years because the region's growth rate will be twice that of the two other principal economic regions—the European Community and the North American Free Trade Area.

The volume of AP foreign trade is already substantial by global standards— currently its share in global trade is about 22 percent compared with 18 percent for the U.S., Canada, and Mexico, and 38 percent for the EC (more than half of which is intraEuropean trade)—and the AP trade share can be expected to increase dramatically in the coming decade. The reason is that imports usually are highly responsive to income growth. Since the AP region's growth will be the world's highest, trade and investment access to its rapidly expanding markets will be among the world economy's principal engines of growth. Consequently, such access—or impediments to it—will increasingly dominate the world's economic agenda during the next decade.

In its dealings with the Asia-Pacific economies, the U.S. will confront large issues that can be lucrative or costly depending on how they are resolved. They will probably be at least as difficult as those that have afflicted the nearly concluded six-year negotiations of the Uruguay Round of the General Agreement on Tariffs and Trade (GATT). The issues relating to soybeans and oilseeds, that have entailed so much acrimony in U.S. relations with France, are relatively "small potatoes" by comparison with those that will arise in economic relations with the AP region in the coming decade.

U.S. economic relations with the AP countries will confront pervasive as well as subtle forms of neo-mercantilist policies—not less formidable than those that have occupied center stage in the GATT arena and in negotiations between the U.S. and the EC. In addition to the use of subsidies to sustain and encourage high-cost agricultural production—the standard pattern of protectionism in Europe—the AP countries practice dual-pricing policies (for example, domestic prices of Japanese and Chinese consumer goods are substantially higher than the corresponding dollar prices of the same products typically charged in foreign markets by Japanese and Chinese producers). Also, the AP countries often use tax rebates to encourage exports, tax surcharges to discourage imports, arbitrary customs classifications, as well as restrictions or outright exclusion of certain categories of services or commodity imports (for example, foreign-made cars in Korea), and foreign investments in certain economic sectors.

Although all of these issues have arisen in prior U.S. trade negotiations with Europe and in GATT, their frequency and prominence are likely to grow as their principal venue shifts from Europe to the AP region. Within the AP region, U.S. relations with China will be of growing importance, as well as complicated by two special considerations. First, during 1993, it is likely that China will be admitted to GATT. Because GATT members accord most-favored-nation (MFN) status reciprocally and automatically to other members, the U.S. will be hard pressed to deny this status to China once it becomes a member of GATT. As a result, leverage on China's human rights behavior, that the U.S. has exercised by its annual consideration of whether or not to grant China MFN access to the U.S. market, will be lost, or at least weakened.

Second, China's rapid overall economic growth has been and is likely to continue to be accompanied by substantial increases in its military spending, force modernization, and purchases as well as sales of weapons and military technology. Indeed, China is the only major power that is still increasing its military spending substantially. Whether and how this enhanced military strength will be used may pose serious problems in a world that increasingly adheres to the view that military strength is decreasing in importance relative to economic strength.

In the coming decade the AP region as a whole will require more of the time and attention of U.S. policymakers, and, within the region, China is likely to warrant increasing emphasis.

13. Arms, Trade, and a Less Disorderly World[14]

One enduring aspect of the "old" world order that will seriously impede emergence of a "new" one is the international market for conventional, but often technologically advanced, arms: aircraft, tanks, artillery, surface-to-air missiles, surface-to-surface missiles, and naval ships. Hyperactivity in the arms market will hinder, if not defeat, efforts to sustain stable military balances in various regions of the world and to create and maintain a less disorderly world. It is also likely that arms trade may become a delicate issue in relations between Russia and the United States—perennially the two largest suppliers in the arms market.

In the last years of the 1980s decade and the start of the 1990s, the volume of transactions in the international arms market was between $45 billion and $50 billion annually. Perhaps this enormous volume will decrease in the years to come. Iraq's enormous purchases of arms in the 1980s have been discontinued if not terminated. And the buying power of other Third World arms importers will probably be restricted by soft prices and reduced earnings from oil exports, competing demands to finance internal economic development, and generally tight conditions in the international capital market.

However, other factors may act in an offsetting direction to sustain a high level of activity in the arms market. On the supply side, these include the growing pressures in the defense industries of the United States and other supplier countries to expand exports and thereby partially compensate for declining defense budgets and domestic procurement. On the demand side, the stimulus will come from the recurrence or emergence of ethnic and irredentist conflicts in the Middle East, Eastern Europe, South Asia, and elsewhere that will boost the demand for weapons by potential buyers.

---

[14]A slightly abbreviated version of this essay was published under the title "Arms Transfer: A Trade That Needs Policing" by the *Wall Street Journal* on March 16, 1992. Reprinted by permission of The Wall Street Journal, © 1992 Dow Jones & Company, Inc. All Rights Reserved Worldwide.

In recent years, the former Soviet Union was the largest arms seller with about 40 percent, or $20 billion, in annual worldwide sales. Only a third of this amount, about $6 billion, represented hard-currency sales—the remainder was typically financed by soft, long-term ruble loans, which have been and are likely to remain unrequited. Still, even at this level, arms exports were the second largest source of hard-currency earnings of the former Soviet economy, exceeded only by export earnings from oil and natural gas. The United States has been the second largest seller with about 20 percent of the global total, or $10–11 billion annually.

In October 1991, the five principal arms suppliers (the so-called "first-tier" suppliers)—France, China, the United Kingdom, the United States, and the then-Soviet Union, now principally Russia—agreed upon a nonbinding arms trade protocol. The agreement provides for the maintenance of a current registry with full information about arms exports by the G-5 suppliers, as well as for serious efforts to restrain this trade. Specifically, the signatories have agreed to avoid weapons transfers that would "aggravate an existing armed conflict . . . increase tension . . . or introduce destabilizing military capabilities." Aside from its other limitations—notably, its nonbinding character, and its emphasis on good intentions rather than enforcement mechanisms—the October protocol is impaired by its failure to consider the so-called "second-tier" arms suppliers, notably Brazil, India, Israel, North and South Korea, as well as others. Restraint by the main suppliers, should it occur as a result of the October protocol, might actually encourage rather than discourage the second-tier suppliers to fill the breach.

The ensuing competition may be further abetted by the agendas of potential arms importers. In the absence of effective means of stabilizing regional military balances, prospective arms buyers in the Middle East and elsewhere may actively seek arms imports from second-tier suppliers to substitute for weapons systems that may become harder to obtain from first-tier suppliers. Moreover, it is by no means clear that the first-tier suppliers will in fact curtail their arms exports.

There are other considerations that make this entire scene even more worrisome. As the U.S. defense budget declines, spending on procurement, which has typically been about 30–35 percent of total defense spending, will encounter particularly severe constraints. As a result of recently announced policy changes by the Department of Defense, more emphasis is to be placed in future defense budgets on research, development, test, and evaluation (RDT&E), and less on procurement, with a view to building so-called "shelf" capabilities, rather than deployed ones. Procurement orders will probably be for relatively small production runs. As a consequence of these new policies, incentives will be strengthened for defense industry firms to look toward sales abroad as a means of defraying the fixed costs of development and the smaller production runs at home. Similar pressures impend in the other principal supplier countries. In sum, arms producers are likely to devote increased efforts to stimulating the demand for their exports, as well as to obtain government subsidies for them.

These circumstances present particularly complex choices and challenges for Russia, and to a lesser extent Ukraine and Kazakhstan, as the principal arms producers of the former Soviet Union, and for U.S. policy toward them. As President Yeltsin pursues serious marketization efforts, the Russian economy's need for hard currency will be compelling. And Russia can be presumed to have a comparative advantage in weapons exports relative to its other potential export sectors. As a consequence, U.S. policy toward Russia and the other republics is likely to face a difficult and awkward dilemma. One option would be simply to accept Russian competition in the international arms market, with the expectation that higher-performance American weapons will predominate in the marketplace, as they did against Soviet equipment fielded by Iraq in Desert Storm. However, while American suppliers in the arms market may now feel confident that their established clients in the Middle East and elsewhere will continue to prefer American jet aircraft, ships, tanks, and air defense and strike missiles to Russian varieties, the progress of marketization in Russia may make the Russian brands competitive on cost and quantity grounds in the future.

The other direction for American policy is to endorse and try to enforce binding limitations on global arms trade, in the process incurring political opposition from our own afflicted defense industrial firms, as well as probable breaches and evasions by firms and governments of the other supplier countries.

The first choice—competition among arms sellers abroad, especially Russia, the United States, and other first- and second-tier sellers—will add fuel to the fires of instability that smolder in various regions of the disorderly world. The second choice—undertaking serious efforts to establish, monitor, and enforce vigorous collective controls over arms exports and imports—will face serious political opposition at home and abroad, as well as considerable risk of failure because of the powerful incentives operating in both exporting and importing countries to expand the arms trade, regardless of formal agreements.

For the "new world order" to have a chance of being less disorderly than the one it supersedes, the second course of action is the more promising road to travel.

There is another important reason for endorsing this second approach. With dissolution of the Soviet Union, the United States faces few if any adversaries with the capability to provide their own military equipment. Rather, adversaries that the U.S. may encounter in possible future regional conflicts will depend almost entirely on the international weapons market to meet their needs. Hence, control or regulation of that market offers the possibility of significantly limiting the extent to which there are nations capable of posing threats to vital U.S. interests if intervention became necessary to protect them. For this reason, too, developing mechanisms for such control and regulation should be an essential component of U.S. strategy for the new world order.

14. Demystifying the Japanese Mystique[15]

Six hundred years ago, an English cleric, William of Occam, proposed a fundamental principle to guide philosophic inquiry. Subsequently called "Occam's razor," the principle stipulates that simple explanations and answers should be preferred to complex ones; complexities should only be introduced when simple explanations have been proven inadequate.

Occam's razor is also helpful in non-philosophical realms. For example, it can be usefully applied to answer the familiar and troublesome questions about the performance and competitiveness of the Japanese economy: its relatively rapid growth, its aggressive development of high-technology industry, its large and continuing export surpluses, and the economic "threat" it is said to pose to U.S. "competitiveness."

All of these issues can be understood and accounted for by simple explanations without recourse to the more complex ones invoked by such commentators as Chalmers Johnson, Karel Van Wolferen, James Fallows, Clyde Prestowitz, and Pat Choate in expressing their often strident criticism of Japanese policy and urging adoption of a countervailing American one. The targets of their criticism include Japan's industrial policy, the special role of MITI, the prevalence of collusive Japanese business practices, *keiretsu* industrial organizations, tariff and non-tariff trade barriers, discriminatory regulatory and contractual practices, and finally, Japanese culture and society.

Notwithstanding that there is some truth in these allegations, most of the explanation for Japan's formidable economic record and challenge lies elsewhere. It lies in four simple, dominant, and straightforward facts, some of which are likely to be transitory.

---

[15]A slightly abbreviated version of this essay was published by the *New York Times* on May 26, 1991. Copyright © 1991 by The New York Times Company. Reprinted by permission.

The first is Japan's high rate of aggregate domestic investment—averaging about 24 percent of its GNP in the late 1980s, compared to a rate of about 16 percent in the United States.

The second is Japan's still higher rate of domestic savings—averaging about 28 percent of its GNP in the late 1980s, compared to a figure of only 13 or 14 percent in the United States.

The third contributing factor is a highly disciplined, trained, industrious, and literate Japanese labor force. And the fourth is an energetic, competent, and experienced management that has learned, through exposure to intense domestic and international competition, to strive continually to raise product quality and cut production costs.

The first of the four facts accounts for nearly all of the difference in average annual growth rates—about 2 or 3 percentage points—between Japan and the United States. It also largely explains Japan's particularly strong performance in certain specific sectors—for example, automobiles, consumer electronics, and semi-conductors—which are capital-intensive or R&D-intensive.

The first and second facts, taken together, account for Japan's persistent trade surpluses (which are explained by the excess of its domestic savings over its domestic investment rate); they also account for the persistent trade deficits of the United States (the excess of its domestic investment over domestic savings).

And the third and fourth factors account for Japan's generally more rapid growth of productivity—although this is more arguable than the preceding inferences.

In the next five years, Japan's savings rate is likely to fall somewhat as a result of rising consumer demands and a population whose proportion of elderly people is increasing more rapidly than that of the United States and other industrialized countries. Japan's investment rate may also decrease as a result of tighter capital markets and a reallocation of resources from the private to the public sector. For similar reasons, Japan's productivity growth will probably also decrease in this time period.

It is difficult for the United States to boost its savings rate, but tax policies provide one means of doing so: for example, by allowing for partial deductibility of interest income, while reducing the tax deductibility of interest payments. If the United States wants to raise its investment rate, reduction of capital gains taxation would also be warranted—although here too, political feasibility and economic desirability collide.

These comments do not invalidate the complaints and criticisms that have been made by the critics mentioned earlier. Nor does it follow that the United States should forgo applying strong and persistent pressure, through Super 301 and other means, to level Japan's economic "playing field."

For example, it is increasingly inappropriate and aggravating that Japanese restrictions impede efforts by American firms to establish manufacturing plants in Osaka or Nagoya, or that formal and informal restrictions prevent foreign firms from trading on the Tokyo stock exchange, or that American engineering and construction firms should find innumerable, often subtle obstacles placed in the way of submitting competing bids and being fairly judged in contract awards. And it is anachronistic for the Japanese to invoke the outmoded shibboleth of "food security" to justify their opposition to agricultural trade liberalization through GATT.

Persistence of these practices is galling to the American public and the Congress, demeans Japan's international standing, and harms the broad relationship between the United States and Japan. Like the spectacle of tax-cheating by the rich, beggaring one's neighbor is especially offensive when practiced by those who are economically strong. However, application of Occam's razor suggests that such objectionable practices probably account for a very small part of Japan's impressive economic accomplishments and its prominent and powerful position in the world economy.

15. Clintonomics *Versus* Reaganomics[16]

President Clinton's State of the Union message to the Congress on February 17, 1993, defined a broad economic agenda for the nation, as President Reagan's had done 12 years earlier. Like the debate that ensued over Reaganomics, the impending debate over Clintonomics will deal as much with politics as with economics. But in other respects, the character of the Clintonomics debate will be strikingly different.

During the early Reagan years, the economic debate was principally between those *inside* the administration, or very closely linked to it—Martin Anderson, Robert Mundell, Robert Bartley, Jack Kemp, and Jude Wanniski—and those *outside*—including many mainline economists in academia. For the most part, it was also a debate between Republicans and Democrats. The Clintonomics debate will be no less a debate between those *inside* the Clinton administration than between them and those outside, including the Republicans. Moreover, the debate's agenda will be notably different.

The Reaganomics debate of the 1980s focused on monetary policy and supply-side economics. (The "Laffer-curve" argument—that reducing tax *rates* might result in increasing tax *revenues*—was a component of supply-side economics.) Protagonists of Reaganomics asserted that both corrective monetary policy and new supply-side policies were essential and, moreover, that the neglect of supply-sideism was a yawning gap in standard economics. The response of the standard economists was that monetary policy was unreliable and that supply-sideism and Lafferism, while admittedly novel, were just plain wrong! (On the issue of novelty, both sides of the debate erred: these ideas had been advanced in detail decades earlier by Joseph Schumpeter, in a neglected monograph on the *Crisis of the Tax State*.)

---

[16]This essay was published under the title "Us Against Us" by *World Monitor The Christian Science Monitor Monthly* in April 1993.

The new debate over Clintonomics focuses on fiscal policy, rather than monetary policy, pitting fiscal "activists" against fiscal "conservatives" within the Clinton entourage. Notwithstanding their differences, the contending sides agree on two core propositions that set them apart from the protagonists of Reaganomics: that government (especially the federal government) should play a more active role in guiding the economy, and that defense spending should be cut by more than the 20 percent reduction already planned over the next four years by the Bush administration. Thereafter, the two sides within the Clinton administration diverge sharply.

The "activists" consist of two groups: old fashioned Keynesians (like Nobel laureates, Robert Solow and James Tobin), who advocate a fiscal stimulus to the economy through increased government spending to boost aggregate demand, employment, and industrial capacity utilization; and the program activists, who are less concerned with aggregate spending than with increasing outlays on particular programs and sectors that they favor—for example, "infrastructure," health insurance for the uninsured, housing, education and training, environmental protection, community development, and advanced technologies. This group includes the corresponding cabinet heads—Donna Shalala, Robert Reich, Federico Pena, Henry Cisneros, Carol Browner—and Laura Tyson in the Council of Economic Advisors. They may differ with one another over program priorities but can be expected to make common cause with the Keynesian activists in promoting what they believe is needed to reduce one or another aspect of the nation's so-called "investment deficit." However, the Keynesians' influence will continue to be weakened if the economy's considerably improved economic performance in the second half of 1992 continues.

Both groups of fiscal activists focus mainly on government spending, while giving less attention to taxation. To the extent they address taxation issues, their emphasis is usually on distribution and "fairness," rather than supply-side incentives—that is, increasing taxation of upper-income groups and corporations, while reducing it for lower- and middle-income recipients.

In opposition to the fiscal activists are the fiscal conservatives within the Clinton administration. Their concerns focus on the overriding need to reduce the federal budget deficit from its current level of 5 percent of the gross domestic product. Among the fiscal conservatives are the Secretary and Deputy Secretary of the Treasury, Lloyd Bentsen and Roger Altman, the Director and Deputy Director of the Office of Management and Budget, Leon Panetta and Alice Rivlin, and the Chairman of the National Economic Council, Robert Rubin.

The fiscal conservatives on the Clinton team use a collage of valid, invalid, and arguable propositions to support their view of the pernicious effects of large deficits, and the important reasons for reducing them: for example, to ease the pressure of government borrowing on bond markets and on interest rates (valid); to reduce the burdens imposed on future generations by current fiscal imbalances and the growing national debt (invalid, because these burdens largely represent payments *to* future generations of bondholders, as well as *by* future generations of taxpayers and lenders); to avoid or ease the "crowding out" of private investment and the depletion of private savings (partly valid, depending on whether deficits are reduced by cutting spending or raising taxes); and to reverse the image of an irresponsible government that is "living beyond its means" (politically valid, economically dubious). Fiscal conservatives also argue that the sort of fiscal stimulus envisaged by the nostalgic Keynesians would be inflationary and ineffective under present conditions, because structural reasons—such as low productivity growth and the trade imbalance— rather than insufficient aggregate demand account for the economy's slow growth. The fiscal conservatives will also be helped by evidence that annualized growth in the last half of 1992 exceeded 3 percent, thereby weakening the case for fiscal stimulus.

When Clinton's fiscal conservatives address tax issues, their inclination is to move toward one or another form of consumption tax—such as some type of energy tax—to encourage saving. (Although partisans of Reaganomics emphasized the importance of strengthening incentives to save and invest, they and others outside the Clinton team have been reluctant to favor consumption taxation because of a fear that its power to generate huge revenues would inevitably whet congressional appetites to boost government spending.)

Both aspects of the debate between fiscal activists and fiscal conservatives within the Administration were reflected in the President's State of the Union address. The eventual outcome of this continuing debate between the insiders, as well as between them and those outside, will ultimately define Clintonomics. Predictably, the result will be a compromise: limited fiscal stimulus (for infrastructure, education, and training) that will increase government spending and will be justified as reducing the so-called "investment deficit"; partly offsetting reductions in both "discretionary" spending (defense) and "nondiscretionary" spending (entitlements, Medicare, and Medicaid); and efforts to use tax policy to slow consumption growth—for example, capping the tax deductibility of employer-provided health benefits, an energy tax, and taxing a larger proportion of Social Security income for higher-income recipients. Clintonomics will be an eclectic mixture of activist and conservative ingredients. It will be less coherent than the supply-side emphasis of Reaganomics, and perhaps also less vulnerable to criticism because most potential critics will find something in the mixture that they like to offset what they don't like. On the other hand, support from potential adherents may be weakened because they find something in the mixture to dislike that offsets what they like.

16. The State of the World—Review of *Seize the Moment* by Richard Nixon[17]

If a contest were held for the best extended essay on the state of the world by a living former president of the United States, Richard Nixon's *Seize the Moment: America's Challenge in a One-Superpower World* (Simon & Schuster, 322 pages, $25.00) would win the prize.

If eligibility were extended to allow participation by former heads of government in other countries, Nixon's book would still be a good bet, but entries by Margaret Thatcher, Helmut Schmidt, and Yasuhiro Nakasone would make the contest closer and more interesting.

Seize the Moment is a *tour d'horizon* of global scope that addresses the current state of the world, where it is heading, and the challenge that these trends portend for U.S. interests and policies. It also presents a challenge to an author who aspires to describe it and prescribe policies that the "one superpower" should follow—a challenge that Nixon meets confidently and competently. That the book's coverage is uneven—generally better in sketching the big picture than the fine-grained details—is not surprising. One might hope that the country does as well in actually meeting the challenges it faces as Nixon does in prescribing for them.

Nixon's ninth book (eight have been published since he left the White House in 1974) begins with an overview chapter on "The Real World"—a title presumably intended as a contrast to the mythological world inhabited by many foreign policy commentators. Nixon takes careful aim at "three myths that [have] dominated the debate about the future of U.S. foreign policy." The first is the "myth of the end of history." (In Nixon's view, the reality is that it is quite premature to proclaim "the triumph of . . . liberal democracy and market

---

[17]A slightly abbreviated version of this essay was published by the *Wall Street Journal* on February 4, 1992. Reprinted by permission of The Wall Street Journal, © 1992 Dow Jones & Company, Inc. All Rights Reserved Worldwide.

economics.") The second is the "myth of the irrelevance of military power." (In reality, "those who propound the irrelevance of military power vastly overstate the influence of economic power.") And the third is the "myth of the decline of America," in contrast to the reality that the United States is "the only country that possesses global economic, military, and political power."

The second and longest chapter deals with "The Former Evil Empire," a subject to which Nixon brings insight as well as experience. His evaluations of Gorbachev ("a Soviet version of Adlai Stevenson") and Yeltsin ("a combination of John Wayne and Lyndon Johnson") are acute, especially so since they were made in September 1991, four months before Gorbachev's resignation as president of the since-dissolved Soviet Union. Nixon forecasts a future in which the republics of the former Soviet Union can be "not only allies, but also friends" of the United States. Toward this end, he calls for direct ties to the republics, strong support for Yeltsin's efforts at comprehensive systemic economic reform, but avoidance of Marshall Plan-type financial assistance. "The greatest contribution the United States could make," he concludes, is "not financial, but ideological."

Seize the Moment then addresses successively Europe ("The Common Transatlantic Home"), "The Pacific Triangle" (China, Japan, and Russia), "The Muslim World," the less-developed countries ("The Southern Hemisphere"), and "The Renewal of America." Although for the most part his broad-brush treatment is sound and well-informed, Nixon's literary style is at times cloyingly didactic and categoric. Besides the "three myths," there are "three dangers" (that "could make the victory of freedom short-lived"), "three fundamental errors," "four fundamental geopolitical facts," "five new realities," "three basic currents of Muslim thought," "three fatal illusions," and "five basic rules" for U.S. policy in the Arab-Israeli dispute!

In the course of Nixon's tour of the world scene, he endorses comprehensive and rapid transformation of the former Soviet republics' economies ("broader implementation of the Polish 'shock therapy' model"), rather than piecemeal gradualism. Advocates of "democratic socialism"—whether in the former Soviet Union or in the West—are a frequent target of Nixon's severe criticism. He sees, but perhaps underestimates, the rising tide of protectionism in the European Community but concludes that "the strategic benefits [of European integration] continue to outweigh the economic costs of rising protectionism." Nixon makes a novel suggestion for how the United States might circumvent this protectionist EC trend. He proposes a two-step process in which the EC grants associate-member status to the East European countries, while the United States forges "a close economic relationship" with them that could "give the United States a potential backdoor into an increasingly protectionist post-1992 Europe."

Turning to Japan, Nixon repeats much that is familiar in recent discussion of U.S.-Japanese economic and political relations. He is neither a "basher" nor an apologist for Japanese mercantilism, urging that "we should not fear but learn from competition." Nevertheless, he would accept, but "only as a last resort . . . selective retaliation if the Japanese refuse to abandon clear and identifiable unfair trade practices."

Nixon's discussion of China and its old-guard leadership is balanced as well as forthright. While favoring increased U.S. economic "engagement" with China, he proposes that we foster political change not only by resuming "high-level dialogue" with the Chinese leadership, but also by opening up two new broadcast stations, Radio Free China, and Radio Free Tibet, "to provide these nations with independent information and commentary." He also proposes condign toughness in resisting and penalizing foreign sales by China of nuclear technologies and missiles, while urging that the United States should "enhance Taiwan's international political standing."

The book's treatment of "The Muslim World" is particularly uneven. For example, he asserts that the "electoral appeal [of fundamentalism] is weak"—a judgment that seems highly questionable in light of the recent Algerian election returns. And he dismisses efforts at regional arms control in the Middle East as both "inadvisable" and "unfeasible," although the reasons he offers to sustain this judgment are arguable, if not wrong.

Turning to "The Southern Hemisphere," Nixon argues for measured U.S. concern and involvement for moral, economic, and security reasons. He excoriates the statist propensities of "Western academics," and strongly and unsurprisingly endorses free markets, human capital investment, limited government tax burdens, foreign investment, and export-led growth as the policy directions that the United States should encourage in the developing world. He is less convinced than many that "democracy is the answer to the underdeveloped world's problems," citing the experience of the four Asian "tigers" as grounds for his doubts.

The concluding chapter of *Seize the Moment* addresses the "renewal of America," providing the usual list of the country's problems—savings, investment, education, crime, drugs, the homeless, and so on. This discussion is longer on rhetoric than it is on solutions. He argues that "birthright entitlements [are] corroding American society," suggesting further that solutions lie in the realm of "values, attitudes, and behavior," and that these are not dependent on dollars.

Nixon concludes with a call for American leadership in a period fraught with opportunities as well as dangers. He endorses for the present era Winston Churchill's statement of 45 years ago that "the United States stands . . . at the pinnacle of world power . . . with primacy in power is also joined an awe-inspiring accountability for the future." And Nixon concludes that "we must seize the moment not just for ourselves but for others."

If Nixon's book is at times as much sermon as it is analysis, he has the fundamentals right. His generally upbeat attitude toward America's opportunities and capabilities provides a refreshing contrast to the "nattering negativism" that abounds in many recent pronouncements by members of the community of foreign-policy experts.

17. Friction-Filled Future for "Big Three"—Review of *A Cold Peace* by Jeffrey E. Garten[18]

In "A Cold Peace: America, Japan, Germany, and the Struggle for Supremacy" (Times Books/Random House, 288 pages, $22), Jeffrey E. Garten argues that disputes and rivalries among the Big Three will dominate international affairs in the next decade and beyond. These confrontations, he writes, will arise over such issues as trade policy and protectionism, foreign investment and industrial policy, immigration and refugees, global alliances and burdensharing.

There is both sense and nonsense in Mr. Garten's views. He is on solid ground in saying that "the international setting (will) be radically different from what we have known," and that the United States can expect to have serious disputes with both Japan and Germany. Among the corroborating indicators are the recent and continuing differences in their respective positions in GATT, on assistance to the republics of the Commonwealth of Independent States, on peacemaking in the Balkans, on coordination of their national monetary and fiscal policies, and on international environmental policies.

Garten also has sensible and original things to say about the reasons "why domestic policy and international policy must be meshed together . . . [because] the foreign policy agenda is so dominated by issues rooted in policies at home— trade, investment, currencies, technological cooperation"; about the different characteristics of capitalism in the three countries (he labels the American system a "liberal market economy," that of Japan, a "developmental economy," and that of Germany, a "social market economy"); and about the differing "degree of openness" in each of the three societies.

---

[18]A slightly abbreviated version of this essay was published by the *Wall Street Journal* on August 12, 1992. Reprinted by permission of The Wall Street Journal, © 1992 Dow Jones & Company, Inc. All Rights Reserved Worldwide.

82

However, Garten's frequent display of good sense and insight is accompanied by equally impressive lapses from them. The lapses are conceptual, empirical, and judgmental.

One conceptual flaw inheres in a framework that, by its preoccupation with the *soi-disant* Big Three, accords remarkably little attention to such other major current and prospective players as China, Russia, India, Brazil, Korea, and other regional powers. Notwithstanding the economic and financial scope of the three, the influence of these "n-th" countries is likely to loom much larger in the new and impending disorderly world than Garten acknowledges.

Another conceptual flaw is Garten's implicit presumption of monolithicity in what "Washington," "Tokyo," or "Berlin" does, and represents, or how each will behave, or progress in the future. The reality is more complex and diverse. In each of the three, significant entities and individuals—corporations, professional associations, scientists, financial institutions—may act differently from the simplistic uniformities that Garten attributes to them.

Furthermore, the Big Three also have major common interests, for example, convertible currencies, protection of their sea and air lines of communication, progress toward peace in the Middle East, and toward marketization and democratization in the republics of the former Soviet Union. Such common interests provide a much broader base for cooperation and collaboration among the United States, Japan, and Germany than is envisaged in *A Cold Peace*.

Some of the empirical data scattered throughout the book are erroneous or apocryphal. The United States certainly doesn't "sell or produce" 20 percent of its GNP abroad, as Garten asserts. U.S. exports of goods and services are 8 percent of its GNP, and the only part of foreign production by U.S. subsidiaries that is included in the calculation of GNP is factor income from abroad (about 2 percent of GNP), not their total production.

Another empirical lapse is reflected by Garten's statement that with respect to shouldering "greater global responsibilities . . . Tokyo and Berlin are unlikely to move one inch more than they have to." Japan's financial undertakings in the environmental area at the Rio Summit in June 1992, and Germany's enormous resource transfers to Russia and the other republics are counter examples.

The judgmental flaws in *A Cold Peace* frequently occur because the author is captivated by the many writings of recent years that bemoan the problems and shortcomings of the U.S. economy, and that forecast the decline of American power and influence in the world. To be sure, these problems warrant serious attention and careful analysis, as well as sensible remedial actions. But remedying the serious U.S. problems in education, drugs, crime, health costs, and productivity growth isn't helped by an unrelenting disposition to magnify them, while ignoring equally serious, although different, domestic problems in Germany and Japan.

Garten pays little attention to the problems that Japan faces in the aging of its population, the shaken confidence produced by the 60 percent drop in the Nikkei Index, MITI's efforts to enhance "the quality of Japanese life" through a shorter work week and through higher levels of per capita consumption and recreation, probably leading to a more slowly growing economy, although perhaps a happier society.

It is also likely that both the costs and time required for successful German unification have been drastically underestimated, resulting in increased inflationary pressures, a redirection of Germany's exports toward the Eastern länder, a fundamental change in Germany's ability to export capital abroad, and serious stresses and strains in Germany's social structure.

It is no more sensible to underestimate the problems confronting one's competitors than to be complacent about one's own.

DATE DUE

DEMCO 38-297